THE EARL OF ABERDEEN'S RAILWAY

UDNY TO METHLICK

THE GREAT NORTH BRANCH THAT NEVER WAS

DAVID FASKEN

Published by

THE GREAT NORTH OF SCOTLAND RAILWAY ASSOCIATION

Foreword by Lord Aberdeen

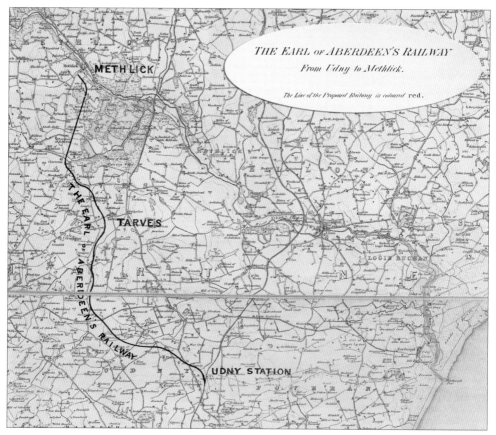

Plan of the proposed route which accompanied William Paterson's plans and sections of the railway.   (Haddo Estate Archive)

Cover Photo: This postcard issued in Great North days shows a busy scene at Oldmeldrum but it could easily have been Methlick if the line had been built. The branch train is ready to depart for Inverurie. The train consists of a couple of 4 or 6-wheeled passenger carriages, a passenger brake, about 4 wagons and a goods brake and is hauled by 'Meldrum Meg', in this case a Cowan 4-4-0.   (Great North of Scotland Railway Association)

© David Fasken 2018
ISBN: 978-0902343-31-3

Published by the Great North of Scotland Railway Association, www.gnsra.org.uk

Printed in the United Kingdom by Henry Ling Limited, at the Dorset Press, Dorchester, DT1 1HD

CONTENTS

Acknowledgements

I am indebted to Keith Fenwick, Keith Jones and Mike Cooper of the Great North of Scotland Railway Association for their invaluable assistance in producing and publishing this book. Mike's photographic skills have brought the original railway plans to life. This was all made possible by Lord Aberdeen who, very kindly, placed the Haddo Estate archives at our disposal and who has supported the project from the outset.

I must also thank Alistair Coull, Director of the Keith & Dufftown Railway Association; Muick Gordon of Methlick who supports Haddo House by looking after and restoring the family vintage train collection; Alistair and Aileen Flett of the North East Aberdeenshire Members' Centre of the National Trust for Scotland; and David Spaven, well known railway author and consultant. They proofread my drafts and responded with very valuable comment and feedback.

As with previous research, I thank the Local Studies Department of Aberdeenshire Council in Oldmeldrum, in particular David Catto, Carole Thomson, and Judith Legg, all of whom responded to my endless requests for sources with a wonderful balance of helpfulness, endless patience and good humour. Between us we unravelled this hitherto untold story.

Finally, I thank Ian Jackson, National Trust for Scotland Senior Assistant Retail and Visitor Services at Haddo House, and his colleagues for their help and support.

Five Great North of Scotland Railway buses and a motor car wait at Haddo House on private hire before World War I. The occasion has not been recorded but it illustrates the important part the Gordon family and Haddo House played in the community.　　　　(GNSRA)

THE EARL OF ABERDEEN'S RAILWAY.
IN THE PARISH OF FOVERAN, IN THE COUNTY OF ABERDEEN.

NUMBER ON PLAN.	DESCRIPTION OF PROPERTY.	OWNERS OR REPUTED OWNERS.	LESSEES OR REPUTED LESSEES.	OCCUPIERS.
1	Loading Bank,	Great North of Scotland Railway Company; Robert Milne, Manager; John Henry Udny, Esq. of Udny, Superior; Thomas Wilsone, Factor for Superior.		Great North of Scotland Railway Company; Robert Milne, Manager.
2, 3	Gravelled Areas between the Goods Sidings,	The same,		The same.
3, 3, 3	Goods Siding Rails,	The same,		The same.
4	Goods Shed,	The same,		The same.
5	Access to Goods Shed and Loading Bank,	The same,		The same.
6	Coal Depot,	The same,		The same.
7	Access to Station,	The same,		The same.
8	Ground Planted with Shrubs,	The same,		The same.
8a	Slope of Railway Embankment,	The same,		The same.
9, 9, 9	Public Road past Udny Station to Pettymuck, and Embankments of same, No. 11 on Classified Road List,	The Ellon District of Road Trustees; George Ferguson Raeburn, Clerk; James Dawson, Surveyor; James Forbes Lumsden, General Clerk to the Aberdeenshire Road Trustees.		
10	Bridge over Railway,	The same.		
11	Garden Ground,	The Aberdeen Town and County Banking Company; George Livingston Rorie, Manager; John Henry Udny, Esq. of Udny, Superior; Thomas Wilsone, Factor for Superior.	William Geils,	William Geils.
12	Arable Land,	John Henry Udny, Esq. of Udny; Thomas Wilsone, Factor.	Andrew Sharp,	Andrew Sharp.
13	Farm Road,	The same,	Alexander Marr and Andrew Sharp,	Alexander Marr and Andrew Sharp.
14	Slope of Railway Cutting,	Great North of Scotland Railway Company; Robert Milne, Manager; John Henry Udny, Esq. of Udny, Superior; Thomas Wilsone, Factor for Superior.		Great North of Scotland Railway Company; Robert Milne, Manager.
15	Main Line,	The same,		The same.
16	Gravelled Area between Main Line and Loop Line,	The same,		The same.
17	Loop Line,	The same,		The same.
18	Railway Border, Waste Land,	The same,		The same.
19	Arable Land,	John Henry Udny, Esq. of Udny; Thomas Wilsone, Factor.	Alexander Marr,	Alexander Marr.
20, 20, 20	Public Road past Udny Station to Pettymuck, and Embankments of same, No. 11 on Classified Road List,	The Ellon District of Road Trustees; George Ferguson Raeburn, Clerk; James Dawson, Surveyor; James Forbes Lumsden, General Clerk to the Aberdeenshire Road Trustees.		
21	Ditch and Waste Border,	John Henry Udny, Esq. of Udny; Thomas Wilsone, Factor.	Alexander Marr,	Alexander Marr.

Extract from the 1880 Book of Reference which accompanied the Parliamentary Bill, showing some of the properties affected.　　　　(Haddo Estate Archive)

FOREWORD

BY THE 7TH MARQUESS OF ABERDEEN AND TEMAIR

Few, if any, modes of transport arouse emotions quite like railways, both from a positive and negative point of view, since the commencement of the major boom in building them in the mid-19th century. Railways have created some of the great feats of engineering over the centuries with fine viaducts, tunnels and tracks which carve their way through some of the most inhospitable parts of the country. The railway bridge over the Firth of Forth remains one of the most iconic symbols of Victorian engineering in the world capable of carrying world famous steam engines of the same classes as *Flying Scotsman* and *Mallard*. The north of Scotland was opened up as a result of such innovation and it created a

network that greatly enhanced the distribution of both people and goods. My family has always been aware of my Great Grandfather's ambition to build a railway from Udny Station to Methlick, principally to help his many farm tenants have an easier method of getting their products to market. He patently took it very seriously as witnessed by the full survey of the land and its owners which would have enabled it to be constructed.

He failed to factor in the opposition of neighbouring business interests who were fearful of the diminution of their own enterprises. This would have come as a shock to him as he was renowned as a gentle and benevolent man and he would have genuinely felt he was only doing good for the farming community both locally and further afield. It is testament that even over 130 years after the event there is a desire to record its history in this excellent, well written and extensively researched booklet. I am delighted that I was able to make available a number of documents that has contributed to its production.

Lord and Lady Aberdeen

Haddo House, a sophisticated Palladian mansion situated just over 20 miles north west of Aberdeen, was built in the 1730s by William Adam for William Gordon, 2nd Earl of Aberdeen. It has seen many changes over the years, especially by the 4th Earl who employed the famous Aberdeen architect Archibald Simpson to enlarge the house. In 1877 the 7th Earl laid the foundation stone for the chapel on the extreme left. The property passed into the hands of the National Trust for Scotland in 1979, although today Alexander Gordon, 7th Marquess of Aberdeen and Temair, and his wife Joanna still live on and manage Haddo Estate.

(David Fasken, courtesy National Trust for Scotland)

INTRODUCTION

This is the tale of a wee branch line in rural Aberdeenshire. It was never built. It was the private project of John Campbell Gordon, 7th Earl of Aberdeen, of Haddo House, and it was planned to run from Udny, south of Ellon on the Buchan railway line from Dyce to Peterhead and Fraserburgh, to the village of Methlick.

This was no spurious plan. It was a professional project, fully appraised and surveyed. The Earl proposed to finance it himself. His objective was to enhance the value of his Haddo Estate and benefit his farm tenants.

What transpired was a furious and unexpected public debate over the winter of 1879 – 1880. There were three protagonists: Lord Aberdeen and his loyal tenants; Mr B.C. Urquhart of Meldrum House and the business community of Oldmeldrum, collectively protective of their own branch line terminus; and the Great North of Scotland Railway Company, who very quickly experienced that sinking feeling when it was expected to operate any new railway.

The debate is played out, largely on an amiable basis of mutual respect, against a backdrop of local self-interest, with a reluctant railway company forced to participate while playing the diplomatic card. The discussions and comments of the time provide a unique insight into local attitudes towards the Great North of Scotland Railway and its services, epitomised by Mr Urquhart's Shakespearean tragedy description of "....that wretched and starving Turriff line".

The background is set with a short summary of railway development in north east Scotland and the opposition of the Prime Minister of the United Kingdom (the 4th Earl) to railway encroachment on his Haddo Estate in the 1850s. The story is completed with the legacy of the aborted project, as the Udny – Methlick route became recognised as an important public bus link, which, rather ironically, was pioneered by the Great North of Scotland Railway. It survives today.

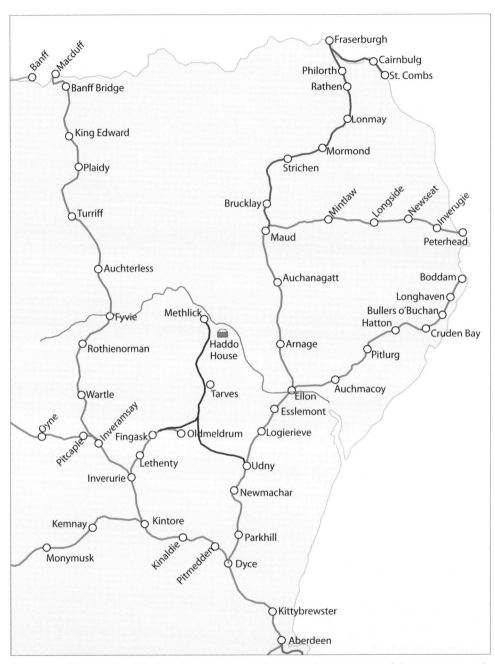

Great North of Scotland Railway lines in the north east with the routes of the two proposals to reach Methlick, one from Udny and the other from Oldmeldrum, shown in red.

GREAT NORTH OF SCOTLAND RAILWAY

Five major railway companies evolved in Scotland in the 19th century – the North British, Caledonian, Glasgow and South Western, Highland and Great North of Scotland. Despite its rather pretentious title, the Aberdeen-based Great North of Scotland Railway (Great North) was the smallest. In 1845 the Highland Railway engineer Joseph Mitchell proposed a direct railway line south from Inverness to Perth over the Grampian Mountains. He was, however, ahead of his time as Parliament expressed incredulity at the projected gradients and firmly rebuffed his proposal.

In the same year, political and business interests in Aberdeen, determined that any railway development in and around the Granite City would be Aberdeen-led, put forward their own proposal for a line to Inverness and this was authorised.

The Great North in Aberdeen and (what was to become) the Highland Railway in Inverness each targeted the other's base in order to control the first north-south route. The Great North opened its main line to Huntly in 1854, but the Highland was already pushing east to Nairn. The result was that the two companies met head-on at Keith in 1858. The 108½ mile link between the Granite City and the Highland Capital was completed, but it was the proverbial "line of two halves" with Keith almost exactly half-way. The Great North did, however, succeed in pushing further west by acquiring two alternative lines, one to Elgin via Dufftown, Craigellachie and Rothes in 1863 (the "Glen Route") and the other via Cullen and Buckie in 1886 (the "Coast Line").

The Great North had a big problem in Aberdeen. The original line to Huntly, having in part used the bed of the former Aberdeenshire Canal from Port Elphinstone to Aberdeen, started and terminated at Waterloo Quay next to the harbour. This was half-a-mile distant from Guild Street, where trains from and to the south arrived and departed. Although a special horse-drawn omnibus connected the two stations, it proved notoriously unreliable, and many passengers were left (or chose) to find their own way. Connections were often missed, particularly when trains from the south ran late. The fractious and often aggressive relationship between the Great North and Highland companies, especially at Keith, combined with the inconvenient transfer and poor connections in Aberdeen, encouraged Joseph Mitchell and his Inverness investors to revisit his direct line south.

The Highland Main Line from Inverness to Perth opened in 1863. That provided a fresh impetus to establish an easier interchange between railways north and south of Aberdeen. In November 1867 a new line through the Denburn Valley, involving two tunnels, linked Kittybrewster directly with a new station adjacent to Guild Street. This immediately effected a great improvement. The station became known to generations of Aberdonians as the "Joint Station" as it was shared, by the Great North of Scotland Railway initially with the Scottish North Eastern Railway, and subsequently the Caledonian. Later the North British Railway used the station.

Unfortunately, the capital investments in the lines to Keith and Elgin and in Aberdeen Joint Station resulted in financial problems for the Great North. The new competing direct Inverness to Perth line hit them hard, especially with the loss of the valuable mail contract. Initially the Great North had a poor reputation for service and its Directors held conflicting business interests in sea freight! All these factors combined to limit the Great North's westward expansion to Elgin and, thereafter, it concentrated on building a network of branch lines throughout the North-East. Indeed the company developed an image of being "all branch line".

These served the coastal communities of Lossiemouth (1852), Banff (1859), Peterhead (1862), Fraserburgh (1865), Macduff (1872), Boddam (1896), and St. Combs (1903); as well as the agricultural centres of Oldmeldrum (1856) and Alford (1859). Ballater on Deeside, in which the Great North had an interest, was served from 1866. Most of these lines were promoted, and indeed built, by small local companies, but they had neither the finance nor expertise to operate them and were, within a relatively short time, absorbed by the Great North. There was a major consolidation in 1866. The conveyance of fish, agricultural produce and tourists complemented the day-to-day passenger business. The railway served dispersed agricultural centres and small market towns and was instrumental in the north east of Scotland developing as a region renowned for fattening cattle. Trains brought in store cattle and fertiliser and conveyed fat cattle to market. In 1866 the Speyside Line connected the Great North at Craigellachie to the original Highland Main Line at Boat of Garten. This line provided another route to the south and served both whisky distilleries and timber operators.

In 1923 all Britain's railways were consolidated into four large companies. This was known as the "Grouping", but even after that the two halves of the Aberdeen – Inverness line were in different camps. The eastern half (Great North) became part of the London & North Eastern Railway (LNER) and the western half (Highland) of the London, Midland & Scottish Railway (LMS).

It was not until Nationalisation in 1948 that the entire line from Aberdeen to Inverness was united under the sole management of British Railways, although it was 1960 before a fast through service was introduced. But Dr Richard Beeching lay in wait. He was the Chairman of the new British Railways Board from 1961 to 1965. From the early 1920s the internal combustion engine had gradually been stealing market share from railways all over the country, and increasing competition from buses and lorries, followed by an upsurge in private car ownership in the 1950s and 1960s, led to people abandoning the railways in droves. Passenger services had in fact been withdrawn from the Oldmeldrum and Boddam lines in 1931 and 1932 respectively; and from the Alford and Macduff branches in 1950 and 1951 respectively. The savage "Beeching cuts" of the mid to late 1960s saw all the remaining Great North branches, without exception, closed to passengers. From 1968 only the original main line from Aberdeen to Keith (and on to Inverness) remained. Services were cut and passenger numbers diminished further. Diesel replaced steam. The double track from Aberdeen to Keith was singled in 1971, apart from a short section between Insch and Kennethmont.

Freight did continue, but at much reduced levels as road competition hit hard. Fish traffic continued on the Fraserburgh – Dyce branch until closure in 1979, while whisky-related goods, mainly barley, were transported on the surviving Keith – Dufftown line until the early 1980s. Timber was moved on the main line until the early 2000s. Since then freight movements have been sporadic, although in 2009 a new freight terminal was opened at Raith's Farm to the north of Dyce station. This has seen limited use to date, but in 2018 it is being used as the base for materials for the doubling of the track between Kittybrewster and Inverurie.

Today, passenger traffic on the original main line flourishes. The burgeoning North

Sea Oil industry led to a boom in industrial and housing development along the route. That, combined with associated road congestion along the A96 corridor and rising fuel prices, has led to a line reborn. Dyce station, closed in 1968, re-opened in 1984. Keith and Huntly stations have been re-built and Inverurie improved. A more regular commuter service in and out of Aberdeen has evolved. The line is today a hard-working railway running at full capacity, serving regular commuters, shoppers and visitors. By 2019 the track between Aberdeen and Inverurie should once again be double and a station is planned for Kintore. New trains, in the form of refurbished Inter-City 125 stock, will offer higher comfort and better on-train facilities.

It is against this background of continual railway development and constant change that successive generations at Haddo House were connected with the railway.

The railway line to Methlick was to terminate above the village in order to facilitate further extension northwards over the River Ythan. The tracks would have ended on the east side of and immediately adjacent to the B9170 road (the mid-photograph fence line) just to the right of centre. The station would have been situated in the field in the foreground. The farm of Little Methlick lies amongst the rolling countryside in the trees to the left. (David Fasken)

Looking towards the end of the line at Oldmeldrum in the 1950s. Traffic had decreased by this time but several motor lorries were still required to serve the surrounding district. The town can be seen in the distance with the hill which faced arriving passengers. If the line had been extended to Methlick a new station to the north would have been built but no nearer to the heart of the village.   (John Emslie/GNSRA)

The epitome of the rural branch line. A G5 0-4-4T No.67287 ambles along the Oldmeldrum branch near Lethenty in July 1952 hauling a modest goods train. The brake van is an ex-Great North vehicle. A few of these ex-North Eastern locomotives worked in the north east in the 1940s and 1950s, after the native 0-4-4Ts were withdrawn.   (J L Stevenson)

Railway Rejected by the 4th Earl in 1858

Initially, railways did not receive much support at Haddo House. After the main line from Aberdeen to Huntly opened in 1854, the first branch line was built from Inverurie to Oldmeldrum only two years later. It was just 5½ miles in length and, being eight miles from Haddo, it was used regularly by the Gordon family for travel to and from the south. This is not that surprising, because the opening of the Oldmeldrum branch immediately led to the withdrawal of the appropriately named horse-drawn coach service *Lord Haddo* between Methlick and Aberdeen from 28th July 1856, less than a month after the first train ran into Oldmeldrum.

However, when the Formartine & Buchan Railway was authorised in July 1858 to construct a new line from Dyce to Mintlaw which would have run east of the house, this was a step too close to Haddo for George, the 4th Earl (1784 - 1860). He refused to allow the section between Ellon and Maud to encroach on Haddo Estate and his objection effectively prevented that railway from serving Pitmedden, Tarves, Methlick and New Deer. The family was descended from the 15th century "de Gordon" family and was known as both "the Haddo" and "the Methlick" Gordons, owning the land in both locations.

In the context of those times this opposition to the railway was a rather surprising position to take, as other local landowners embraced the new form of transport with enthusiasm. For example, Sir Andrew Leith-Hay allowed the main line to Huntly to be constructed through the southern policies of Leith Hall near Kennethmont, although in return he would have received an annual feu duty payment or the land value in capital shares.

Lord Saltoun was another to embrace the railway, allowing the line near Fraserburgh to pass through his estate in return for his own private halt at Philorth.

The 4th Earl of Aberdeen's contrasting position is rather puzzling, especially as he was well travelled. Towns such as Dyce and Maud would, in time, flourish as a direct result of the Buchan line. Indeed the railway led almost immediately to the establishment of the Buchan Combination Poorhouse at Maud which brought a population increase of 150 and to the development of the famous Maud cattle mart. In contrast, Tarves and Methlick missed out and remained relative backwaters. The answer may lie in the 4th Earl's prominence in public life as a leading politician, not least his position as Prime Minister of Great Britain from 1852 to 1855 during which time he oversaw the country's struggle with Russia in the Crimean War. Personal privacy, and indeed security, may have been his priority. However, the 4th Earl of Aberdeen was not the only landowner proving difficult to deal with, as the Formartine & Buchan Railway Company's law agents reported in December 1858 that "*some show a disposition to get the highest terms they can…*". By March 1859 only half of the 24 landowners between Dyce and Mintlaw had accepted a feu duty. It may just have been all down to money and the 4th Earl drove as hard a bargain as anyone else! But, it may have been even simpler than that because, within the family, there is a belief that the 4th Earl simply held an aversion to "*new-fangled things*". In any event, he died in 1860, a year before the Formartine & Buchan Railway opened.

Despite the snub to the new railway,

Haddo did merit a mention in the 1861 tourist guide to the Formartine & Buchan Railway. Visitors were encouraged to walk from Udny (or Culter-Cullen as it was then referred to) to visit the house, grounds and gardens: "*The park is as extensive and varied as any in this part of Scotland*". The guide also made interesting comments about local agriculture: "*One cannot but be struck with the fine farms which lie scattered over this rich district, and the high state of cultivation....Richer pasture we have rarely seen, nor finer and more cultivated fields; whilst the large herds of cattle, of the most approved breeds in the kingdom, which graze in the ample enclosures, at once bespeak the enterprise of the tenants and the liberality of the landlords*". The "*agricultural tourist*" (!) would meet farmers who would leave a marked impression "*....of their urbanity, intelligence, and hospitality*". Sadly, the 4th Earl was not impressed by such "*agricultural tourists*".

He was succeeded by his son George, 5th Earl of Aberdeen (1816 – 1864), who was dogged with ill-health and who died only four years later. He, in turn, was succeeded by his son George, 6th Earl of Aberdeen (1841 – 1870). Concerned by family debt, he elected to avoid his responsibilities and followed a common lumberjack's and seaman's life incognito in America. Eventually, having resolved to face his responsibilities at Haddo he decided to return home, but on the night of 27th January 1870 as First Mate of the *Hera* bound for Australia, he was washed overboard during a storm off Sable Island (Nova Scotia).

This marble bust of George, 4th Earl of Aberdeen (1784 – 1860), sits in the House of Lords. The 4th Earl was Prime Minister of Great Britain (1852 – 1855) during the Crimean War with Russia He refused to allow the Buchan Line to encroach on Haddo Estate.   (Haddo Estate Archive)

7TH EARL'S RAILWAY PROPOSAL 1879

The youngest brother of the 6th Earl, John Campbell Gordon (1847 – 1934) succeeded as the 7th Earl of Aberdeen in 1870 and he took a keen interest in railways throughout his life. He held an affection for the Great North of Scotland Railway from the days of his youth when he enjoyed cab-rides and engine-driving lessons on the Oldmeldrum branch. The branch locomotive was known to locals as 'Meldrum Meg'. He served as a director of the Great North from 1884 until 1906, being deputy chairman from 1900. Years later the Earl recalled his first footplate experience in the summer of 1862 during the Royal Northern Agricultural Society Show in Aberdeen:

> "There was a vast attendance, and all the trains were over-crowded, including the branch train from Inverurie to Old Meldrum, whither I was travelling home. The lack of space in the train, of course, furnished a good excuse for resorting to the engine, where I was at once made welcome by the engine driver, Peter Anderson. That was the beginning of much enjoyable experience…."

Shortly afterwards Sir James Elphinstone, then Chairman of the Great North of Scotland Railway, was lunching at Haddo House:

> "Immediately after the meal I approached him, with due deference, asking if I could have permission to travel occasionally on the engines. In reply he at once declared, "I'll give you a pass which will enable you to go on any engine in Aberdeenshire." Those who can remember Sir James can imagine the breezy heartiness with which he would make this utterance. Forthwith he sat down and wrote the following:

> "Permit the Hon. John Gordon to ride on any engine of the Great North of Scotland Railway and Branches." How gratefully I received and carefully cherished this talisman! And the use of it was quick and constant; indeed, if it had been produced on every occasion of such use, it would soon have been in shreds and tatters."

Lord Aberdeen was soon well-known to many of the company's engine drivers whom, he recorded, treated him "with the greatest kindness and indulgence on the railway." His experiences soon extended beyond the Oldmeldrum branch on to the main line into Aberdeen. One day on approaching Kintore, while the train was in motion with the steam cut off, and on his own initiative, he moved along the outer bearings of the locomotive in order to oil the cylinders (normally the job of the driver or fireman). On his return to the cab Driver Anderson commented that the Earl could take his place while he took a day's holiday, although he was quick to remind him that he was still only an apprentice as he had allowed the wind to take his hat! Two other favourite drivers were men called Thompson and Tom Howie and the Earl copied the latter's distinctive way of sounding the locomotive's whistle. He became so proficient that one day while on the footplate on the approach to Udny on the Buchan line, and still out of sight of the station, his elder brother James waiting on the platform knew his brother was on the engine. The Earl took great satisfaction from his brother's recognition of his particular whistle style; and, in time, his talent for imitating railway whistles became so practiced, often indicating the differences between various lines, that it became his "party *piece"* reserved for children and special friends. Two Prime Ministers, William Gladstone and the (5th) Earl of Rosebery were both known to call for his whistle performance!

The Earl of Aberdeen served as a Liberal Peer in the House of Lords and, given his interest, it was not surprising that he became involved in railway matters. Indeed, in 1873 his maiden speech was on the subject of railway safety and the following year he was appointed Chairman of a Royal Commission examining railway accidents. In 1879 the Earl, determined to make up for his grandfather's earlier opposition to the railway, proposed a *"light railway"* be constructed from Udny to Methlick (then spelt "Methlic"), which lay close to Haddo House. The parish of Methlick then boasted a population of over 2,000. After sending his written proposal to the Great North Board, the news of the new line hit the press on Monday 13th October and clearly was a surprise to everyone.

The railway was surveyed and planned

William Paterson, who planned the line.
(Anne-Mary Paterson)

by the well-known Highland Railway civil engineer, William Paterson of Inverness, and was drafted by Keith & Gibb of Aberdeen, *"Draftsmen and Engineers to the Queen"*. Paterson had links to Thomas Telford, being apprenticed to one of his general assistants. He later became both assistant to and partner of the famous Highland Railway pioneering engineer, Joseph Mitchell.

There were only two landowners involved – Mr Udny of Udny and Lord Aberdeen himself. At this time Lord Aberdeen's land extended from New Deer to the bridge over the railway at Udny Station, and from the Boat of Ardlethen to Crichie. The proposed route meandered somewhat in an attempt to avoid costly over-bridges as much as possible:

"Leaving Udny with a moderate curve towards the north, it would continue for about ¾ mile on the property of Mr Udny of Udny. Passing beneath the public road (from Aberdeen to Tarves, Methlic, etc.) the railway would then come upon the Earl of Aberdeen's property, and continue on it throughout the whole of the remaining portion of the route. Passing to the north of the farm of Tillymaud, the line would run with an easy descending gradient past Green of Udny towards Tarves (crossing the Oldmeldrum and Newburgh road between the farms of Cairnbrogie and Cairdseat), and then continue in an almost direct line to Tarves, a convenient site for a station being available close to the village on the west side. The line would then pass by the farm of Nethermill to Keithfield, which would be another suitable point for a station. The remaining portion to Methlic would be direct, but with some rather heavy cutting. The approach to Methlic would be with an easy curve towards the north, in such a manner as to enable a prolongation of the line to be made without difficulty should such, at any future time, be found desirable; and

A southbound train entering Udny station in the early years of the twentieth century. If the branch to Methlick had been constructed, the platform on the left would have been widened and a new track constructed on the other side of it.   (GNSRA)

the last ½ mile, including the station yard, would be on a gradient of only 1 in 500."

Apart from Udny and Methlick, three intermediate stations were planned, the first between Udny and Tarves, the most convenient location for passengers being considered to be between the farms of Cairnbrogie and Cairdseat. After the second station at Tarves, the third was planned for Keithfield to serve Haddo House, close to the entrance to the West Approach and about 1½ miles from the House itself. A grand new lodge and other improvements had recently been made there. Methlick itself was seen as the centre of Lord Aberdeen's estate and, in itself, of a large and important agricultural district. Despite being relatively remote from the railway system, agriculture and related business was increasing.

The estimated cost of £55,000 comprised:

Earthworks	£13,000
Bridges, culverts, etc.	£11,000
Permanent Way, fences and gates	£17,000
Roads, including metal and fences	£ 2,000
Stations, sidings and signals	£ 7,000
Contingencies	£ 5,000
Total	£55,000

Compensation for land was not included but as there were only two landowners involved, the Earl himself and Mr Udny, who agreed to allow the line through his estate, this was not a significant issue. The Earl would also cover this. However, the original estimate was higher than anticipated because surveys had thrown up considerable amounts of rock through numerous ridges and also due to the large number of roads to be crossed. On the plus side, Lord Aberdeen considered the time was right because the price of labour and materials was cheaper than in previous years. And, with agriculture having been depressed in these years, he was anxious to provide a public improvement to help his own tenant farmers. He had recently re-let many of his farms on new 19-year leases with no rent break-clause as he strived to offer a degree of stability for his tenants.

The outcome was the preparation of a Parliamentary Bill for the first Session in 1880. It included full surveyed plans of the line, including a *"Book of Reference"* listing those who would be affected along the way. The official notice of the Parliamentary Bill was completed on Monday 10th November 1879 and was published in the *Edinburgh Gazette* on Tuesday 18th November. It was drafted jointly by Tods, Murray, & Jamieson, W.S. of 66 Queen Street, Edinburgh and C. & P. H. Chalmers, Advocates, of 13 Union Terrace, Aberdeen as Solicitors for the Bill. Martin & Leslie of 27 Abingdon Street, Westminster were the Parliamentary Agents.

Notice was served for the application to Parliament for an Act which would incorporate a new Company; allow a new railway to be built in the County of Aberdeen; allow the Great North of Scotland Railway Company both to subscribe and to work the line and make other arrangements with the new Company (including running powers); and confer certain powers to the Earl of Aberdeen in relation to the new railway. The proposed

Act would allow for the inclusion of *"proper stations, works, and conveniences connected therewith…."*. The project was summarised as follows:

"A Railway commencing in the parish of Udny by a Junction with the Formartine and Buchan Branch of the Great North of Scotland Railway at a point on that branch one hundred and fifty yards or thereabouts, measuring along that branch railway in a southerly direction from the south end of the Station House at Udny Station, and terminating at or near the village of Methlick, in the parish of Methlick, in a field belonging to the Earl of Aberdeen, and in the occupation of Alexander Duncan, and numbered 1094 on the Ordnance Survey of Aberdeenshire, which intended railway will pass from, in, through, or into, or be situate (sic) within the several parishes and places following, namely, Foveran, Udny, Tarves, and Methlick".

The notice proposed to bestow on the Company rather wide ranging powers of

Udny in April 1965, looking south from the rear of a northbound train leaving the station. A new bridge would have been required in the embankment on the right for the branch to Methlick.   (J L Stevenson)

compulsory purchase of land and buildings and to allow it to alter or divert existing roads, turnpikes, bridges, rivers and even streets. Nothing was to impede the new line. Critically the Bill would enable the Great North of Scotland Railway to contribute capital, hold shares and appoint directors and it would be allowed to operate its locomotives and rolling stock over the line subject to commercial agreement. The Act would also allow the Great North to manage and operate the entire railway and, if all this sounds rather presumptuous, it must be remembered that this was normal practice for such new ventures in the 19th century. The Earl of Aberdeen could pay for the construction of the new railway, but he would have had little experience or desire to manage it.

Finally, the notice undertook that, by no later than Saturday 29th November 1879, the maps, plans and sections (and the *Book of Reference*) relating to the proposed line would be delivered to the offices of the Principal Sheriff Clerk of the County of Aberdeen in Aberdeen and Peterhead, with copies to be delivered to the Session Clerk of each affected parish "*....at his office or if he has no office at his residence*". Printed copies of the Bill were to be deposited in the Private Bill Office of the House of Commons by no later than Saturday 20th December.

The cover and title pages from the bound book of plans and sections of the line which was prepared to accompany the Bill. The book is 30 inches by 22 inches. These were expensive to produce, each plan having to be engraved for printing. Four of the plans are reproduced on the following pages. These only showed the course of the line and the 'limit of deviation', in effect a corridor through which it could be constructed. Detailed plans were only prepared once an Act had been obtained. The reference to the "*village of Methlick*" provides a significant clue as to why the Great North harboured serious doubts about the proposed line's viability.

(Haddo Estate Archive)

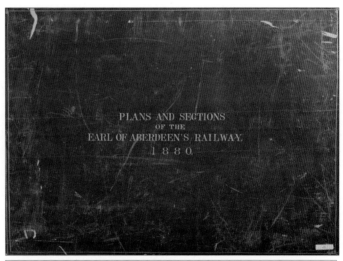

PLANS AND SECTIONS
OF THE
EARL OF ABERDEEN'S RAILWAY.
1880.

THE EARL OF ABERDEEN'S RAILWAY.

PLANS AND SECTIONS
OF THE
PROPOSED LINE FROM UDNY STATION
OF THE
GREAT NORTH OF SCOTLAND RAILWAY
TO THE
VILLAGE OF METHLICK.
SESSION. 1880.

WILLIAM PATERSON, ENGINEER.

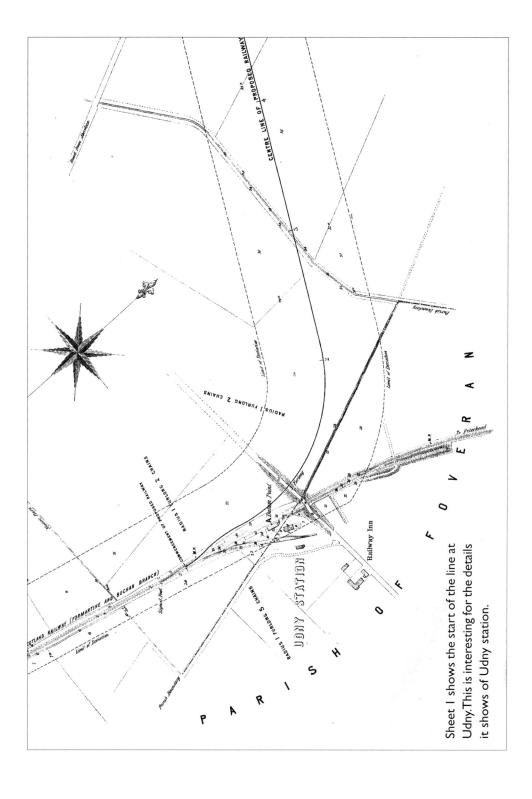

Sheet I shows the start of the line at Udny. This is interesting for the details it shows of Udny station.

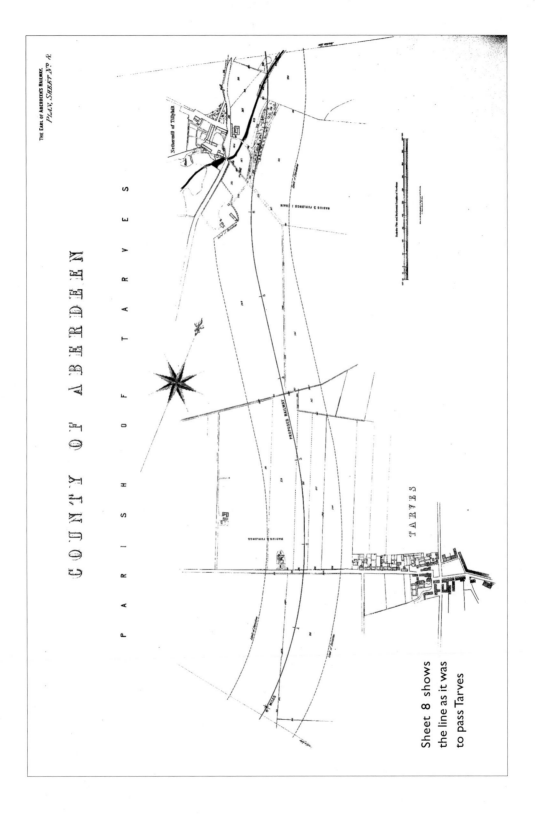

Sheet 8 shows the line as it was to pass Tarves

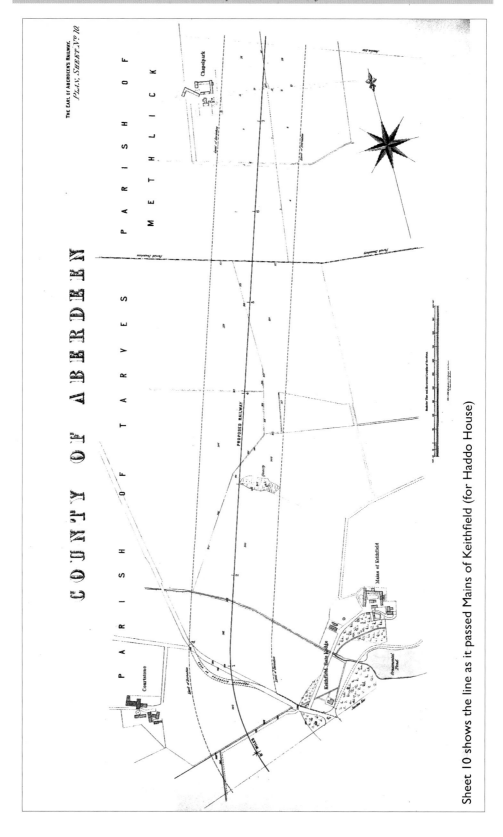

Sheet 10 shows the line as it passed Mains of Keithfield (for Haddo House)

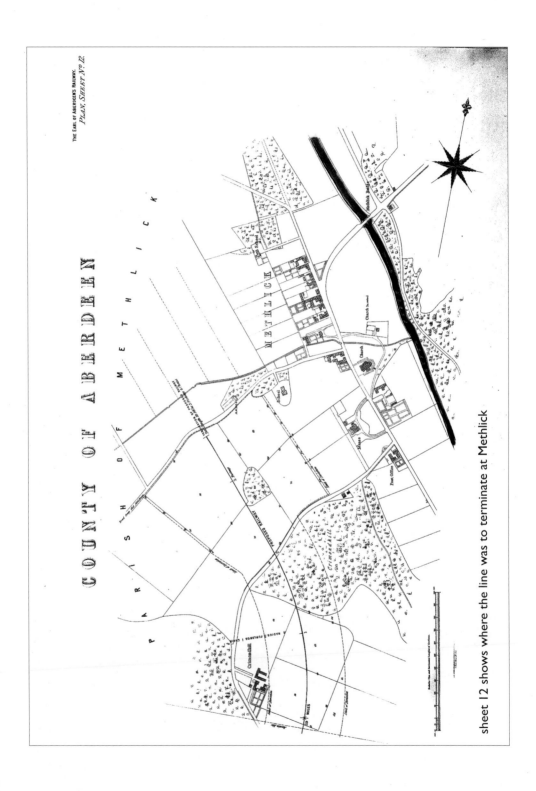

sheet 12 shows where the line was to terminate at Methlick

The lodge guarding the Western Approach to Haddo House has changed remarkably little since its construction in 1878. The dormer windows in the roof have been added, the metal gates have disappeared, and the vegetation behind the house now obscures the farm cottages in the background, but which still exist relatively unchanged today. The proposed station at Keithfield (for Haddo House) was planned to be a couple of hundred yards to the west of the lodge and today's Formartine restaurant and shop (behind the photographer) where the line crossed the B9170 road to Methlick. The distance from Udny was just over 8 miles.

(Upper photo Haddo Estate Archive, lower David Fasken)

Oldmeldrum Opposition

There were two immediate and significant implications arising from Lord Aberdeen's announcement. Firstly, by offering to finance the entire construction cost himself, the Earl had quite astutely placed the Great North in a rather delicate position. A degree of diplomacy was required on their part as the company was already saddled with a substantial number of unremunerative branch lines. Negotiations were planned to discuss the Great North working the line, and Lord Aberdeen turned up the heat by stating he would be prepared to agree to terms which would guarantee the Great North against loss in return for a fair share of any future operating profits arising from growth in traffic.

The second implication arose, rather unexpectedly, from the direction of Oldmeldrum. While the proposal was undoubtedly greeted with much enthusiasm in the immediate country areas, it was met with a high degree of concern and dismay from those with interests in the Oldmeldrum branch. They saw the threat of their railway's existing business being harmed by the new line. Lord Aberdeen believed his railway would generate new business without harming Oldmeldrum and he was confident that both Methlick and Tarves were capable of generating such new business. It is clear that Lord Aberdeen underestimated the reaction and opposition from Oldmeldrum. Almost immediately, on Wednesday 22nd October, a public meeting was convened in Oldmeldrum Town Hall not just to discuss the Udny – Methlick threat, but to consider an alternative plan in order to protect their interests, namely the extension of the Oldmeldrum Railway to Methlick. The meeting was called by leading local businessmen – James Manson, bank agent; James Bruce, banker; John Davidson, merchant; James Hardie, merchant; and James George, draper. The splendidly-named Mr. Beauchamp Urquhart of Meldrum House, the main local landowner, was appointed Chairman and Mr. Alex Stuart Wilson as clerk to the meeting. The involvement of Messrs. Urquhart and Manson (who lived at Fingask) was not surprising as they had been Chairman and Vice-Chairman respectively of the independent Inverury and Old Meldrum Junction Railway Company from 1855 to 1866, which was at this point absorbed into the Great North. The Hall was "*well filled*" and from the start it was clear that Oldmeldrum was up for a fight!

Mr Urquhart had, in advance of the meeting, written to the Chairman of the Great North, William Ferguson of Kinmundy, to request that the Great North Board postpone any decision about Lord Aberdeen's proposal until the Oldmeldrum interests had the opportunity to consider their position. Mr Ferguson knew of the meeting, but was otherwise engaged and he issued a mild admonishment to Mr Urquhart for not having invited Lord Aberdeen to explain his proposal to the meeting. Mr Ferguson and his Board were clearly flummoxed by Lord Aberdeen's proposal: "*You can see that the footing on which Lord Aberdeen places his scheme – namely, the complete construction at his own sole cost – takes his proposal entirely out of the ordinary category of railway extensions*". That being the case, Mr Ferguson concluded that "*the Great North Railway has really nothing to say*".

However, he was equally diplomatic in offering his view that an alternative scheme from Oldmeldrum might also well serve Haddo Estate and the general public. He did point out that it was a greater distance of four or five miles before such a line would reach Haddo. He then rather diluted this encouragement by stating: "*....it is well that you should know prior to your meeting that the directors of the Great North will certainly listen to no proposal which shall involve them in the finding of funds*". Mr Ferguson politely confirmed that his Board would listen to any future communication from Oldmeldrum, either by letter or by deputation, and he even offered to meet Mr Urquhart at his Aberdeen office or "*at the club there*" (presumably his sanctuary from the daily pressure of running a railway company!).

Mr Urquhart was reassured that no concrete proposal had yet been made by Lord Aberdeen to the Great North and that the Great North was being even-handed in listening to both parties. He then turned his attention to considering Lord Aberdeen's proposal, but, rather bizarrely, immediately admitted that "*....we have the very vaguest and scantiest information vouchsafed to us*" (the Public Notice for the Parliamentary Bill was still some weeks away). A major concern was the location of the first station near the farm of Cairnbrogie, which was within three miles of Oldmeldrum. It made little sense to construct a third line northwards in parallel with the Turriff Railway to the west and the Buchan Railway to the east. Methlick was only about eight miles from either line. Lord Aberdeen had written to Mr Urquhart on Tuesday 21st October, although the latter had only received his letter an hour and a half before the meeting. In that letter Lord Aberdeen stated he would have been glad to attend the meeting and that it was only on Tuesday 7th October (when he had met Mr Urquhart in Aberdeen) that he had discovered the concern in Oldmeldrum, as he was firmly of the belief his new railway

would generate entirely new business. He understood that Methlick folk used Arnage, and that Tarves people used Udny at present.

Lord Aberdeen clarified his position. Despite his proximity to Oldmeldrum, he could not support the Oldmeldrum extension because of his own Udny – Methlick railway proposal. He believed that his proposal would be of greater benefit to the district, not least because most passengers would prefer Udny to the much longer journey to Aberdeen via Oldmeldrum and Inverurie. Udny would suit his Haddo tenants. While conceding that some fears of damage to trade in Oldmeldrum might be valid, his line would undoubtedly provide benefits to those on his estate, and indeed increase its value. He pointed out that if the Udny – Methlick railway did not materialise, then Oldmeldrum was highly unlikely to pursue its project, as there was nothing to benefit them. Oldmeldrum already had its railway. He was confident of support from the Great North, as they would have a "feeder" to their current system which would be unencumbered by "*....those burdens and responsibilities with which their other connections were, for the most part, received, and which, no doubt are, to a considerable extent, the cause of the comparatively unfavourable state of the Great North's funds at present*". Lord Aberdeen concluded that he did not share the current gloomy view of the Great North's future prospects, that his new railway would benefit the entire area and that Oldmeldrum would share those benefits.

Notwithstanding the business case for his railway, there was clearly a degree of embarrassment on the part of Lord Aberdeen because he had often used the Oldmeldrum branch in the past and had made many good friends in the town. That element of embarrassment was reciprocated by Mr Urquhart who responded with a note of acknowledgement, in which he apologised for not inviting Lord Aberdeen to the meeting, as despite the mild rebuke from the Great North

Chairman, they thought the most respectful course was to request Lord Aberdeen to receive a deputation following the meeting. He concluded: "*I think I can assure your lordship that the kind feeling you express for the inhabitants of Oldmeldrum is cordially reciprocated by them….*".

The Oldmeldrum group was not swayed by Lord Aberdeen's arguments. While conceding that some Methlick trade went via Arnage, a huge amount of agricultural trade was conducted at Oldmeldrum. That included the collection of large quantities of manure and feedstuffs as well as the despatch of grain and produce from Oldmeldrum station. Tarves was equidistant from both Udny and Oldmeldrum and the latter's share from that village would be threatened by the new line. The group also believed that the Buchan line had enough on its plate struggling to provide a satisfactory service to its existing customers. Interestingly, Mr Urquhart, rather unwittingly albeit indirectly, agreed with Lord Aberdeen on the point of any Oldmeldrum extension not being in the local interest. He admitted that the loss of Oldmeldrum's status as a "terminus" would be injurious and that any extension would not benefit the Great North shareholders, Lord Aberdeen's tenantry, or the general community. At this stage the Oldmeldrum faction appeared to be playing into Lord Aberdeen's hands.

However, there followed a detailed discussion on route mileage. The Oldmeldrum extension was planned to Auquhorthies (2 miles) and on to Tarves (4 miles) where it would join Lord Aberdeen's proposed route. This would give a total Methlick – Oldmeldrum mileage of 8½ miles, which would be 2¼ miles shorter than Methlick – Udny. While Udny to Aberdeen was 14½ miles, Oldmeldrum to Aberdeen was 20½ miles. This meant that the mileage to Aberdeen was only 3¾ miles longer by Oldmeldrum. This additional mileage could not be ignored, but the Oldmeldrum group felt that the Great North could negate

this "*either by acceleration of trains, if there is such a word in the vocabulary of the Great North, or by an adjustment of rates, of which there are a number of precedents in the Great North system*". Basically the group wanted trains via both Udny and Oldmeldrum to arrive in Aberdeen at the same time for the same fare. That would make it a matter of indifference to Methlick and Tarves folk as to which route they used, although the statement did hint at a more fundamental issue in the speeding up of trains! At this stage too, the group conveniently ignored the issue of changing trains at Inverurie and whether the Great North would operate a direct Methlick – Aberdeen service.

However, having ignored the issue of changing trains for Aberdeen at Inverurie, the Oldmeldrum faction introduced a related issue – "*cross communication*" for the north. At present passengers on the Buchan line had to travel to Dyce and on to Inverurie. The Methlick – Udny line would not change that for Methlick people, who would face a journey of 29 miles to Inverurie via Dyce, but only 12½ miles via a new line by Oldmeldrum. A 17 mile saving and when this was put to the meeting it was greeted with much applause!

Mr Urquhart turned to capital cost. Although it was Lord Aberdeen's concern, the extra mileage to Udny was estimated to result in an additional £10,000, while the difficult junction at Udny, due to the gradients, another £10,000. There would be ongoing cost implications for operating this junction, which would prevent "*cross communication*" to the north. Also, the Oldmeldrum line and extension could be worked with "*existing plant*". By now Mr Urquhart was constantly banging the drum about how all this must be of grave concern to shareholders of the Great North! He introduced another theme. He pointed out that the Methlick branch would only connect with another branch (at Udny) of the Great North, and that other branch was single-line. A line from Methlick to Oldmeldrum would create one single branch line to Inverurie on the Great North's main line, which was soon to be doubled into Aberdeen (it was doubled by 1882). After receiving more applause for this argument, Mr Urquhart then attacked Udny as "*the most inconvenient and hampered station on the whole Buchan line*", and questioned the cost to both Oldmeldrum interests and Great North shareholders if business was transferred to that point. He asked who would pay this cost and, after asserting that the interests of both Oldmeldrum and Great North shareholders were inextricably linked, he rather bizarrely turned on the shareholders and directors: "*Whether we can get them to see it in time (the cost implications) is a different thing. We know perfectly that the past history of the Great North has shown that the directors have not always been alive to their own interest*".

Another issue was considered. Where was the line to go after Methlick? "*Is it to go on to Fyvie, and prove that the 'Gordons have the guiding of it' to feed and support that wretched and starving Turriff line?*" Alternatively, the line could extend nine miles to New Maud (as the present-day Maud was then called) via New Deer or to Auchnagatt, which would provide a line of "*cross communication*" and benefit a wider range of Haddo tenants to a far greater extent than the current proposal. Lord Aberdeen's New Deer and Buchan tenants were in danger of losing out and a through line to Auchnagatt or New Maud "*....would produce a direct, strong, and good result; whereas if the line is to be carried through Methlick on to Fyvie it prevents any cross communication taking place*". Udny had simply been chosen by Lord Aberdeen because it was the nearest possible point to the south to reach. Mr Urquhart concluded by stating that Oldmeldrum faced "*utter extinction*" in the face of "*preconceived notions*" and "*foregone conclusions*". One cannot help but conclude that Mr Urquhart was a master of exaggeration!

Mr James Manson, banker, then moved: "*That the meeting, fully recognising*

and appreciating the liberality and the public spirit of the Right Hon. The Earl of Aberdeen in promoting at his own cost a railway to afford accommodation to the Methlick and Tarves districts, is of opinion that a line of railway on the route indicated in the scheme recently published will do very serious injury to the trade and prosperity of Oldmeldrum, and that an extension of the existing railway from Oldmeldrum via Tarves to Methlick, while of equal service to these districts, will not injuriously affect existing interests, and will be more for the public advantage".

Mr Manson felt that, since the railway to Oldmeldrum was first proposed (in the 1850s), there had never been a matter of such vital interest for the district to consider, but he counselled that impartiality was required ahead of individual interest. In that regard any such railway must be for the benefit of the general public and, if that was the case, it would have the full support of the town and district of Oldmeldrum. The problem was lack of detail, but he hoped Lord Aberdeen would listen to local opinion and concerns. Mr Manson was clearly uncomfortable to be put in a position where he appeared to be antagonistic towards Lord Aberdeen. He felt Lord Aberdeen was acting with the best of intentions and that he had forged strong bonds with the people of Oldmeldrum over the years. He believed that the relationship between Lord Aberdeen and his tenantry with Oldmeldrum could be strengthened further if Lord Aberdeen altered his line from Udny to Oldmeldrum. No one could question his motives (in wanting to benefit his estate and tenants), and indeed no one had the right to question his private initiative, except for the fact that his private capital investment would become a public railway under sanction of the Board of Trade and would affect public interests. That gave the people of Oldmeldrum the right to a say in the matter, although he stressed this must be on a "friendly" basis on both sides. Mr Manson was a clever banker (unlike today's fools!), because not only was he urging Lord Aberdeen to switch his support to the Oldmeldrum extension, he was also hinting strongly that he should bring his cash with him. He knew there was no chance of the Great North funding the capital cost of any new branch line and, if Lord Aberdeen did not switch his funding along with his support, he could already hear Oldmeldrum extension promoters knocking on his bank's door!

Mr Manson agreed that a station at Cairnbrogie was a major concern. Freight cost from that point to Aberdeen via Udny was bound to be cheaper than via Oldmeldrum. This, he stated, would cause *"great injury"* to Oldmeldrum. However, he went further. He felt that business would also be diverted to Methlick from both Fyvie on the Turriff line and from Arnage on the Buchan line, thereby adversely affecting both those railways. He also believed that Oldmeldrum's current status as a *"terminus"* gave them an advantage as a *"centre of business"* for a relatively wide area. There was an argument not to build any extension, as Aberdeenshire was already well served by existing lines. He did not believe that it was in the interests of the Great North and its shareholders to expand further. He was, however, careful to concede that, if it was in the general interest, Methlick could replace Oldmeldrum as the terminus, and that the line could even be extended to New Maud. He further conceded that no major engineering difficulties would be encountered between Oldmeldrum and Methlick.

The difference in mileage between Methlick and Udny against Methlick and Oldmeldrum was immaterial to passengers, who were only interested in time and money. Furthermore, the route to Udny only served the south while a route to Oldmeldrum and Inverurie served

both south and north (to which there was considerable traffic). Mr Manson concluded, therefore, that it would make sense to take the Oldmeldrum – Methlick extension on to Auchnagatt or New Maud. This would bring the entire district into direct communication with the north and would allow cross-traffic from Peterhead and Fraserburgh access to Inverurie, Huntly and beyond. This would lead to considerable cost savings to north-bound traffic (i.e. towards Elgin, Inverness and beyond) from Peterhead, Fraserburgh, and other north-east towns and villages. All Aberdeenshire's branch lines converged in parallel lines in the direction of Aberdeen and the proposed Methlick – Udny line would only add another in an area already well served.

Mr Manson's motion was supported and seconded by Mr John Davidson. In doing so, he pointed out that a carrier was already going to Methlick direct from Oldmeldrum, as well as to Cromlet, Mill of Fochel and Barthol Chapel. He could only assume Lord Aberdeen was unaware of this. The resolution was then put to the meeting and unanimously accepted.

Mr James Bruce then moved:

" That an earnest representation be made without delay to the Earl of Aberdeen of the injury that would be inflicted on Oldmeldrum by the line indicated in the published scheme, and of the advantages of an extension of the Oldmeldrum line, with the view of inducing his lordship to adopt the scheme of an extension of the Oldmeldrum line; and that a similar representation be made to the directors of the Great North of Scotland Railway...."

He further moved that a committee be nominated to undertake these deputations. Mr James Hardie, merchant, seconded the motion and the meeting unanimously approved it.

Staff posing in front of a locomotive at Oldmeldrum, in the 1920s. From the left, the second man is a guard and the third is the station master, with his superior uniform. Fourth left is a young woman who was presumably employed in the booking office. The driver is fifth from the left with the fireman standing behind him. The other staff, all less well dressed, were most likely employed in the goods yard.   (GNSRA collection)

The good folk of Methlick would have faced a stiff climb of fully 400 yards from the foot of the village up School Brae to their station. Strangely, Oldmeldrum had the same issue in reverse with the station at the bottom of the village.   (David Fasken)

THE GREAT NORTH DECIDES

In the days which followed, the directors of the Great North considered their position. At the end of that month (October 1879) they threw their support behind the Oldmeldrum group. They stated that they were attracted by the prospect of *"cross communication"* if the Oldmeldrum branch was extended to Methlick. That opened up the possibility of extending further to meet the Buchan line at Auchnagatt, which would provide a through line connecting Peterhead and the north. In fact, they had played a very clever card. The Great North had already made it crystal clear that they would not (indeed could not) finance any further branch lines. By supporting Oldmeldrum they hoped to force Lord Aberdeen to switch his financial support to the Oldmeldrum extension proposal or, alternatively, withdraw. If the latter, the Oldmeldrum group would either have to raise the cash to build their line themselves, or drop the project. However, as the debate developed, the Great North came clean that there was another strong reason for considering the Oldmeldrum – Auchnagatt connection. This "through" route would provide an alternative to the Buchan line whose steep gradients limited goods trains to a load of 25 wagons compared to 50 on the main line. The cost savings of operating a new line of relatively easy gradients would be considerable, and the Great North proposed to switch *"a great quantity of their Peterhead and Fraserburgh traffic"*. Lord Aberdeen wasn't so naïve to think he wouldn't still be targeted for a financial contribution. What the future implications of this strategy would be for the Buchan line is a matter of speculation, but undoubtedly this was being discussed by the Great North Board. After all, the directors were still only at the stage of considering the various strategic options.

The directors, under the Chairmanship of Mr Ferguson of Kinmundy, duly received the deputation from Oldmeldrum and a visit from Lord Aberdeen on Thursday 30th October in Aberdeen. Mr J. Murray Garden, advocate and factor for the estate of Meldrum, and Mr Manson of Fingask made the case for the alternative proposal to extend from Oldmeldrum to Methlick. Later, Lord Aberdeen and his factor, Mr Douglas, outlined their scheme.

However, a third scheme was then presented to the directors by Patrick Barnett, the Great North's Chief Engineer. He proposed to branch off the Oldmeldrum line at Fingask (two miles west of the town and where there was a halt with a simple platform); run to the north of Fingask House partly over the farmland of East Fingask, on to the north of the farmhouses of Whitfield; through the glebe between the Episcopal church and manse; and cross over the Oldmeldrum – Drum of Wartle Road. It then would pass along the Den of Gower to meet Lord Aberdeen's property at Foresterhill, which was about four miles from Fingask and two miles from Oldmeldrum station. A new station for Oldmeldrum was proposed at this point with, presumably, the current station and two mile section from Fingask closing. The line would then run to Craigdam, passing south of the United Presbyterian Church and along the valley to Tarves, where it would cross the road into the village at a slightly closer point than that proposed by Lord Aberdeen. From there to Methlick the Great North would roughly follow Lord Aberdeen's proposed line, but on higher ground. At Methlick the line would cross the Ythan by a new viaduct, cross the road near the church and continue in a straight line to Skilmafilly. It would then run on by Inkhorn, the Church of Savoch and South Mains of Auchnagatt to a terminus and junction with the Buchan line at Auchnagatt. The line's length would be 16 miles from Oldmeldrum (18 from Inverurie). The cost of the line was estimated at £7,000 per mile and there would be no gradient greater than 1 in 100. This compared with some gradients of 1 in 75 on the Buchan line and, despite increased costs for cuttings, the objective was to switch goods traffic. The distance from Methlick to Aberdeen was six miles greater than Lord Aberdeen's scheme, but the new route would take advantage of the new doubling of track between Inverurie and Aberdeen and would allow passengers north of Auchnagatt direct access to the north (i.e. towards Elgin, Inverness, etc.). Not only that, but Peterhead folk would be able to take a "*day return*" to Inverness for the first time, by catching a proposed departure at 06.00am to connect with the 07.00am. departure from Aberdeen at Inverurie. Similarly, passengers from Keith could take the 06.10am train to Inverurie and on to Auchnagatt, arriving at 09.30am to connect with the first train of the day from Aberdeen to Peterhead and Fraserburgh. Mr Barnett dangled a carrot for Lord Aberdeen by explaining that this proposal covered a far

greater area of his estates than his own scheme, especially between Methlick and Auchnagatt which was not covered by Lord Aberdeen's line. The length of railway on Lord Aberdeen's property was 13¾ miles, four miles more than in the original scheme. And he pointed out that no place between Udny and Tarves (excluded from the Great North proposal) was more than 2½ miles from the current railways. Stations were planned for Oldmeldrum, Auquhorthies, Tarves, Keithfield, Methlick, and Skilmafilly, all being roughly equidistant throughout.

There followed a difference of opinion between the Oldmeldrum group and the Great North, with the former claiming that the Great North had pinched their proposal from their meeting on 22nd October . They were pleased, however, to note that their scheme had been endorsed "*….by so competent an authority as Mr Barnett*". There was some confusion as to whether there were now two or three schemes. Oldmeldrum now claimed that the Great North Chairman had intimated, after their meeting, that the directors were supporting the Oldmeldrum to Methlick route, as outlined at the Oldmeldrum meeting, in preference to Lord Aberdeen's scheme.

By now, the Great North was not short of public advice for the railway's route. One suggestion was that a route from Methlick to Maud via New Deer would benefit a wider range of both the general public and Lord

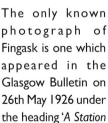

The only known photograph of Fingask is one which appeared in the Glasgow Bulletin on 26th May 1926 under the heading '*A Station without a Staff*'. The Great North Chief Engineer, Patrick Barnett, proposed to branch northwards from the halt to Methlick and Auchnagatt.

Aberdeen's tenants. Another proposal was for the Oldmeldrum extension to join the Buchan line at or near Logierieve, between Udny and Ellon, and continue the line on to Newburgh. It was pointed out that none other than Mr Urquhart, Chairman of the Oldmeldrum group, had recently collected a cargo from that port by cart. A railway to Newburgh would give local farmers an alternative port facility (to Aberdeen) for grain and fertiliser; and a passenger service from Newburgh to Aberdeen would replace the two daily coaches currently operating, with much improved comfort and safety. The land required for such a line would be of low agricultural value (apart from Lord Aberdeen's and Mr Udny's) and it was pointed out that Lord Aberdeen's grandfather (the 4th Earl) had mooted a connection to Newburgh during the "*fight in the fifties*" when the route and construction of the Buchan line was proposed.

As the Provost of Inverurie was criticised for supporting a line to Methlick, because it was really none of his business, the farming interests in Daviot (to the west of Oldmeldrum) broke their silence. They were encouraged by Mr Barnett's through line proposal to Auchnagatt, which would open up the Buchan sea-ports. These would offer "*....terms more advantageous than the pretty heavily-burdened port of Aberdeen....*". They conceded that Lord Aberdeen could not be expected to contribute to the increased cost of a through line, but they suggested that the Oldmeldrum business community offer £5,000 which was the estimated cost of one mile. Another proposal emerged to abandon the route to Auchnagatt via Skilmafilly, but instead branch north-west from Methlick to Mill of Ardo and Mill of Gight, then run due north via Asleid to north of Cairnbanno before striking due east to New Deer to join the Buchan line at Maud. This would provide a route equidistant from Fyvie and Maud, albeit slightly longer and circuitous, which would serve a wider area currently isolated from railways.

The terrain through which the line would have passed, looking north from Keithfield towards Methlick. Although it would have followed a straight path towards the left side of the trees, deep cuttings would have been required here.   (David Fasken)

Lethenty was the only full station on the Oldmeldrum branch. It served an adjacent mill and originally had a small platform and presumably wooden building by the level crossing in the distance. The station was rebuilt just after the First World War, one of the last such investments on the Great North.   (Norris Forrest)

The goods train in the siding at Lethenty in 1959. The turntable in the foreground gave access to the mill. The 7th Earl complained to the Great North about delays experienced by passengers caused by the shunting of wagons on mixed trains.   (Norris Forrest)

LORD ABERDEEN AND HIS TENANTS RESPOND

The ball was firmly back in Lord Aberdeen's court and he convened a meeting of his tenantry on Monday 3rd November in the Melvin Hall in Tarves. Lord Aberdeen took the Chair and nearly 350 tenants attended, a testament itself to the importance of the issue. He started by confirming he had been contemplating his Udny – Methlick railway for a number of years and that his recent proposal had been met with universal support from his tenants. However, some *"difficulties"* had arisen and before proceeding further he deemed it wise *"....to obtain an expression of opinion from those who are chiefly concerned, and whose interests, which are inseparably connected with my own...."*. He made it clear that it was not his intention to issue a lengthy address, but to listen to the views of his tenants.

Before proceeding further, he lightened the tone by stating that he had that morning received a letter which commenced: *"Fat's a' the steer aboot Auldmeldrum?"* Amidst much laughter Lord Aberdeen went on to say that the gentleman who had written the letter had forgotten to sign it! There was a serious point to this, however, because Lord Aberdeen had received a well-signed petition of support from his tenants concerning the grumbles from Oldmeldrum. He made it clear, however, that the Oldmeldrum concerns were not the reason for convening the meeting. It was now a simple choice between his Udny – Methlick *"branch"* proposal and the alternative of the Oldmeldrum extension to Tarves and Methlick, with the further prospect of a *"through"* connection to Auchnagatt on the Buchan line. Lord Aberdeen now referred to the latter option as the *"Great North scheme"*

as he believed that the objectives of the Great North and the Oldmeldrum group were now one and the same!

Mr Thomson, Haddo, and Mr James Hay, South Ythsie, both spoke highly of Lord Aberdeen, who they considered to be their "landlord", and stated that he and the railway project had the universal support from the estate. The benefits would accrue to generations to come. Lord Aberdeen was greatly encouraged by this expression of support, but it was Mr Marshall, Skilmonae, who focussed the meeting by moving:

> *"That this meeting is of opinion that the new scheme of railway extension from Oldmeldrum by Tarves and Methlick to Auchnagatt is far from being the best fitted to enhance the interests of the Earl of Aberdeen's tenantry or facilitate the traffic of the district".*

In support of his resolution in relation to the Haddo Estate, he questioned the *"circumbendibus"* nature and additional mileage of the Oldmeldrum – Auchnagatt route compared to the direct line from Udny to Methlick. Railway rates were based on mileage and he understood a new station would be built at Skilmafilly and, if he and his neighbours were to use that to travel to Arnage, it would be the equivalent of paying a fare from Mintlaw or Longside. It would be cheaper to use horse and cart to and from Arnage. He concluded by reiterating that Methlick to Aberdeen via Udny would be far shorter than via Oldmeldrum.

Mr Mitchell, St. John's Wells, seconded the motion and he questioned the capital cost of the Methlick – Auchnagatt section. He estimated this at £80,000 due to the necessary construction of a viaduct over the Ythan and that there would only be one intermediate station (Skilmafilly) which was equidistant at only three miles to both Auchnagatt and Arnage. New business there would be limited. As for "*through*" traffic further to the north and beyond Inverness, there was none apart from "*a day or two after the herring season*". Fyvie, Methlick (and Keithfield) and Auchnagatt stations could well serve that district and he thought the entire proposal was not rational. He could see no new business arising from a northerly extension from Methlick and believed that Oldmeldrum was better served as a branch line terminus. At this point Lord Aberdeen stated that the Great North had indicated they were prepared to guarantee that rates from Methlick and Tarves via Oldmeldrum would not be greater than from Udny, although they had given no indication of how long they would maintain such a guarantee. Alternatively, higher rates could be countered by speeding up of certain trains.

Mr John Marr, Cairnbrogie, raised the issue of the proposed station on the Newburgh turnpike close to his farm. The Oldmeldrum – Methlick line would eliminate that and exclude around 2,500 acres of farmland from any new line. Farms in that area were, on average, about five miles from Udny and, "*....owing to the extravagant charges made at Oldmeldrum.....they used Udny to a man*". The line to Auchnagatt would be of no use to them and Mr Marr teased Lord Aberdeen by concluding that he would rather have a station at Cairnbrogie than have his rent reduced by £20!

Mr Duthie, Tarves, thought it would be useful to compare some of the present goods rates from Udny and Oldmeldrum, the most important points leading to Aberdeen. He reckoned that 99 out of 100 customers gravitated towards Aberdeen to only one heading north and, therefore, the rates to/from Aberdeen were of paramount importance. Comparisons quoted (per ton) were as follows:

	Udny	Oldmeldrum
Barley and oats	3s/8d	5s/7d
Manure	2/6d	3/9d
Oilcake/bran/feedstuffs	3/8d	5/6d
Coal	2/8d	4/8d
Lime	2/6d	3/9d

The differential was of grave concern to everyone, not least the cost of bringing in feedstuff. Mr Duthie stated that everyone was aware that there had been no thought of new railways at all until Lord Aberdeen had announced his proposal; and that the words from Oldmeldrum were "*an echo of the protectionist theory*". This was the more ironic as Oldmeldrum's railway was partly supported by the businesses of Haddo Estate. What would Lord Aberdeen do if a new merchant set up business in Tarves? Call a public meeting to protect themselves? Mr Duthie doubted it, and he declared the Oldmeldrum protection rather "*curious*" as Lord Aberdeen was being asked to protect the Oldmeldrum people against himself! Mr Duthie received much applause, amidst laughter, for his remarks. He questioned the Great North's support for a line right through to Auchnagatt, while he believed that the Oldmeldrum branch was currently unprofitable. Such a line might be useful if there was no alternative, but Lord Aberdeen was proposing a more natural and cheaper route which had the support of the Tarves folk.

At this point Mr Marshall's resolution was put to the meeting by Lord Aberdeen and was carried unanimously on a show of hands, not one being raised against.

That was not the end of matters as Mr John Grant, Methlick, moved another resolution:
"That this large meeting, so well representing the tenantry on the Haddo House Estates, regard the scheme of railway first proposed by Lord Aberdeen, that from Udny, as in every way best

fitted greatly to benefit not only his lordship's tenantry, but the whole district through which it would pass, and as sure to create a new and large traffic to the Great North of Scotland Railway".

The village and parish of Methlick were well represented at the meeting and Mr Grant assured Lord Aberdeen of the widespread support in that area for his railway. The greatest disadvantage of the through route was the additional mileage. The general feeling was that the area between Methlick and Auchnagatt was already well served by the Buchan line. In any event, the Great North had made it clear it would not fund any extension and there was no indication of alternative funding from elsewhere. Mr Davidson, Mains of Cairnbrogie, seconded Mr Grant's resolution and added a very interesting comment on the Great North's "*hints*" of reduced through rates and accelerated trains: "*These hints were…. looked upon with very great suspicion in the light of their previous experience of the proceedings of the Great North of Scotland directors".* The applause which greeted this assertion confirmed the general mistrust towards the Great North. Again, the resolution was carried unanimously.

By now the Great North was facing questions about funding and had slightly altered their stance. Having declared an absence of funds for branch line investment, they were now actively promoting the Oldmeldrum – Auchnagatt "*through*" route. The Board proposed to raise capital on debentures, secure some additional funds from Lord Aberdeen (presumably to reflect the benefit to his estate), and to find the remainder by public subscription. Lord Aberdeen estimated the cost of the Oldmeldrum – Auchnagatt line to be anywhere between £25,000 and £80,000. If the public's share was between £20,000 and £30,000, the question was whether the public would respond positively. There was little support from the Peterhead area and Mr Copland, Mill of Ardlethen, who declared himself neutral because neither line would benefit him, suggested that, if the people of Oldmeldrum wished a connecting line, they should consider either Oldmeldrum to Ellon or Auchnagatt to Turriff. However, there would be no public funds forthcoming and, if Lord Aberdeen's proposed railway did not proceed, there would be no railway at all. Mr Catto, Mains of Gight, spoke in favour of Lord Aberdeen's railway on behalf of the upper district of the estate and held a list of 50 names of support. This motion was then carried unanimously too. The conclusion was that it would be very doubtful that public subscription would be obtained for an Oldmeldrum – Auchnagatt line.

For many years the GNSR included a list of coaches operated in connection with its trains but outside its control. One journey each way daily was included for the Methlick to Udny route. This typical example is from the May 1892 timetable.

Methlick and Udny Station

Methlick, leave	6 30am	Udny Station, leave	5 50 pm
Udny Station, arrive	8 30am	Methlick, arrive	7 00 pm

John Campbell Gordon, 7th Earl of Aberdeen (1847 – 1934). The 7th Earl proposed to build the new railway from Udny to Methlick in 1879 – 1880. He was created Marquess of Aberdeen and Temair in 1915.

LORD ABERDEEN STEERS A MIDDLE COURSE

Lord Aberdeen's cause was not helped when a letter from the former Great North Chairman Sir James Elphinstone on Tuesday 27th October to Mr B. C. Urquhart, Chairman of the Oldmeldrum group, was published in the local press in early November. Sir James branded Lord Aberdeen's project a "*joke*" and a "*White Elephant*". Sir James, of course, spoke with a very high degree of knowledge and authority, because he had been heavily involved in the entire layout of the Great North network. He stated that considerable investigation and preparatory work had been expended before commercial decisions on new lines were made and he outlined an interesting history of the Oldmeldrum branch. He recognised that this was the only line which was incomplete, but (in 1856) it had been the intention to push northwards to Methlick, and eventually on to both New Maud and Turriff. The objective was to open up the whole centre of that country to the thriving ports of Peterhead and Fraserburgh. That the line stalled at Oldmeldrum was due to the lack of public support in both the Tarves and Methlick areas. In any case, the proposed new line was too close to the existing ones. He had to justify all the new lines before Committees of Parliament, but he would not like to do so for Lord Aberdeen's proposal. It just did not make sense to send Tarves farmers to Inverurie, Insch, Huntly or Keith round by Dyce. He further pointed out that the present railway system had been developed with the "*concurrence*" of Lord Aberdeen's predecessors and, while acknowledging his right to develop his estates to the benefit of his tenants, this must not impact negatively on others. He urged "*strong reason*" and "*mature consideration*".

Three days after the Tarves meeting Lord Aberdeen's Factor, Mr Douglas, met the directors of the Great North. He was accompanied by his commissioner, Mr Jamieson (Jamieson and Haldane, Edinburgh) and Mr Patrick Chalmers, advocate. They confirmed that it was Lord Aberdeen's intention to promote a Bill in Parliament in the next session (in 1880) for his Udny – Tarves – Methlick railway. However, he intended to suspend its operation for 12 months, until the end of November 1880, in order to establish whether an Oldmeldrum – Tarves – Methlick line, with the option to extend to Auchnagatt, or a complete Oldmeldrum – Auchnagatt line, would materialise. If that happened, Lord Aberdeen would abandon his line from Udny. In the meantime he intended to progress his plans. However he undertook that the gradients between Tarves and Methlick would be no greater than 1 in 100, so that it would meet the Great North's requirements for "*through*" as well as "*local*" traffic. The *Aberdeen Journal* reported: "*The directors of the railway company, we believe, gave the deputation to understand that they would offer no opposition to Lord Aberdeen's Bill, provided everything in it is satisfactory*". If that indeed was their response, it did, in fact, mean absolutely nothing! However, the Great North also offered to work it, but subject to certain conditions; and they undertook to discuss both respective rates and train times from Udny and Oldmeldrum. If the Oldmeldrum project was to proceed, the Great North agreed to promote it and Lord Aberdeen agreed to contribute. At this point there appeared to be an even-handed understanding between the Great North and the other two parties.

Sir James may well have regretted his strong words of condemnation because, in the days which followed, he attracted a rash of criticism in response. These are rather neatly encapsulated by a clearly disgruntled Great North shareholder:

> *"I admit that at the outset Sir James Elphinstone was of some use in helping on the formation of the Great North Railway, although of course there were much abler and more practical men with whom the real work lay....The plain matter of fact is Sir James Elphinstone was simply the titled figurehead who officiated as Chairman of the Great North, while men possessed of steadier energy carried forward the scheme of branches....the general result was a system difficult to*

> *work and pecuniarily disastrous to not a few shareholders".*

Quite clearly this was a man who did not mince his words and he accused Sir James of *"huge blundering"*, in particular in respect of the Strathspey branch. He bitterly recalled his words before the opening of the through main line all the way from Aberdeen to Inverness in 1858 – that the *"poor shareholders"* would benefit from the *"circle of locomotion"* – conveniently avoiding the burning issue that this was only achieved in conjunction with the *"Highlanders"* and, as a result, the dream of an entire Great North through main line was *"annihilated"*. He concluded with a very firm put-down: *"And this is the man to lecture Lord Aberdeen and his tenantry on the proper route to follow!"*.

The terminus at Oldmeldrum was at the bottom of the hill on which the village, which can be seen in the distance, sat. To extend the branch northwards to Methlick would have involved a new route to the north of the village, which would have resulted in Oldmeldrum station being further away.   (GNSRA collection)

LORD ABERDEEN WITHDRAWS

The Great North Board now sat on the proposals until they received a report on the potential diversion of traffic from the Buchan Line and while detailed working arrangements were considered. In mid-December it formally decided not to oppose Lord Aberdeen's Bill, provided that satisfactory working arrangements were agreed. Later, however, the Board received legal advice that it should oppose the Bill as this would take the project before a Parliamentary Committee, which would protect the Great North's interests.

Lord Aberdeen completed all the required preparation for obtaining Parliament's authority, but at the end of February 1880 he wrote: *"The estimated cost of construction, and also the difficulty of making terms of agreement with the Great North of Scotland Railway Company, are so much greater than could have been anticipated, that I have come to the conclusion that the project must be abandoned"*. As the rail project faded, the Earl remitted six month's rental to his farm tenants in recognition of their disappointment and frustrated expectations.

The Earl's tenants responded:
"When in the autumn of last year your Lordship announced the intention of constructing at your sole expense a railway through the lands of Methlick and Tarves to Udny, the primary object of the undertaking being, as we well know, to benefit your tenants, we hail with joy the magnificent liberality thus manifested on our behalf. The completion of the costly scheme, thus projected, would have been, we cheerfully acknowledge, of great advantage to the agricultural interests and general business requirements of that portion of your estates; but, when for reasons we fully appreciate, your Lordship deemed it wise to abandon this scheme, and in lieu of that boon, spontaneously intimated entire remission of the current half-year's rent over the whole of your estates, no words of ours can adequately express the feelings of thankfulness which animated us and our families".

Had the line been built, it would have been useful for timber extraction, as Methlick would have served as a more convenient railhead than either Ellon or Aberdeen.

The scheme was briefly resurrected in 1900 in connection with a proposed hydro-electric power station on the River Ythan, but nothing came of it. Despite discussions between the Great North and the Oldmeldrum interests, that scheme also came to nothing. Also, in 1900, there was a proposal for an electric tramway from Methlick to Logierieve, but this did not get beyond the estimate stage. There is no evidence of Lord Aberdeen having been involved.

Interestingly, in 1879 the Earl of Aberdeen was recorded as one of about 3,000 shareholders in the Great North of Scotland Railway Company. The size of the shareholdings is unknown, but the Earl's co-shareholders represented mostly those with North-East interests, such as farmers, ministers, landowners, grocers, sailmakers, fish-sellers, merchants and even John Adam, pointsman at Maud, who was the only waged employee in the share register. It was probably this connection and his regular use of the railway at this time which prompted a clearly frustrated Earl to complain about delays to trains at

Lethenty, the main intermediate station on the Oldmeldrum branch. These were caused by the shunting of wagons on mixed trains (trains of both passenger coaches and goods wagons). The station served the local mill with a private siding. The Great North proposed to remedy the issue with a new dedicated goods shed, although in practice nothing happened!

In the event, the Earl's Parliamentary Bill was withdrawn primarily because estimates had risen from £55,000 to £80,000. Before doing so, the Earl made one last throw of the dice, Mr Jamieson writing to the Great North outlining a number of pre-conditions for the Bill's withdrawal:

"- the 2.10pm train from Aberdeen for Buchan to leave at 2.40pm or 2.45pm, which Lord Aberdeen thought would be popular in the district, so as to connect with the mid-day train from Deeside.

- trains from Aberdeen to Udny, or at least the one above, to be 'materially accelerated'.

- the awkward approach to the west side of Udny station to be improved.

- a loading bank for carriages to be provided at Udny.

- if Lord Aberdeen decided to purchase a private saloon carriage, the GNSR would provide a site for him to erect a suitable shed at his expense; this carriage to be conveyed at a cost not exceeding the 1st class fare for each occupant.

- improvement of the current First Class carriage provided by the GNSR on a courtesy basis between Aberdeen and Oldmeldrum.

- the re-instatement of the Aberdeen to Keith train which connected at Keith with the mid-day train to Inverness (or similar arrangement).

- Lord Aberdeen's mail bag should be charged at the ordinary parcel rate on the mid-day train to Udny.

- rates for all other traffic to and from Udny should be as favourable as those at other stations on the Great North system."

The main demand, however, was for the establishment of a horse bus service between Udny and Methlick. The bus was to be funded in part by both Lord Aberdeen and the Great North. It is not known if these subsidies materialised, but a bus service did operate in the late 19th century underpinned by the Post Office mail contract, as illustrated on page 37. It is very likely that the bus was in fact that recalled years later by a Dr Munro of Tarves:

"The old Morrison's bus – could they ever forget it? – its old fashioned lamp and never-failing smoking wick and filthy smell, serving not to give light, but merely to reveal the darkness; the holes bored in the floor, supposed to allow any surplus water, or melted snow, to drain away, but serving only too well to let in the cold wind in winter, despite the layer of straw, all too scanty, on the floor, supposed to keep the passengers' feet warm."

The Great North Board agreed to consider these suggestions and remitted them to the newly-appointed General Manager, William Moffatt. Indeed this was one of his first tasks.

THE GREAT NORTH DRAWS A LINE

At the 55th Ordinary General Meeting of the Great North of Scotland Railway Company held on Thursday 25th March 1880 in the Douglas Hotel, Aberdeen, the Chairman, Mr Ferguson of Kinmundy, drew a firm line under the whole episode. He reported that the company directors had been "*much occupied*" during the past six months with consideration of Lord Aberdeen's proposal. He tread a fine line, describing the project as "*noble*" in respect of the potential benefits to the tenants of Haddo, while being careful to reassure his shareholders. The Board, he said, would have supported the project, but only as consistent with the rights and interests of the company's proprietors (shareholders). He confirmed that the Great North would have agreed to the new junction at Udny and to work the line to Methlick "*at simple cost*", in the same way as was undertaken for the Alford Valley Line before its amalgamation. However, given the "*peculiar circumstances*" of the proposal, these terms would have been "*onerous*" to Lord Aberdeen. Combined with rising construction costs, this had resulted in the withdrawal of the Parliamentary Bill. Mr Ferguson did not hide his relief: "*The withdrawal of the scheme is a matter of great satisfaction to us, as in any circumstances another branch railway, in addition to our already too numerous branches, would have entailed a great deal of additional difficulty in the working of our complicated system*".

And so Lord Aberdeen's project bit the dust. If ever there was a clearer conclusion to its failure, it was that last sentence from the Great North Chairman. It is not difficult to conclude that the Great North had achieved its original objective of seeing off the proposed new line.

The posturing over "*cross communication*" was bluff, as the operational benefits of longer trains would not have justified the capital investment and would have been partly negated by longer mileage. The volume of freight to the north was not great. The final proof lies with the Oldmeldrum faction – never heard of again. One can only speculate what might have happened to such a railway line had it been built. A passenger service may well have succumbed at the same time as the one to Oldmeldrum in 1931. That would have been a final irony!

What happened to the 7th Earl? He maintained his interest in the Great North all his life. He became a director in 1886 and in 1900 he was elected Deputy Chairman, a post he retained until he retired from the board in 1906. He was held in the highest regard as a man who treated everyone as equal from senior officials to station staff and footplatemen. He took a particular interest in Aberdeen Joint Station where he was a regular and popular visitor. At the turn of the 20th century the station was in poor condition structurally after over 30 years of constant and expanding use. Traffic had outgrown the size of the station, there was regular late running, and passengers notoriously came into regular conflict with barrow loads of wet fish. The low platforms were slimy due to the large number of fish trains passing through. It was a difficult place in which to work, but in the early 1900s proposed reconstruction was afoot.

The Earl also gave public credit to the Great North for the introduction of the "First and Third only" concept to Britain's railways. It had adopted this system of passenger class since the first main line to Huntly was opened in 1854 and it was later experienced by Mr Ellis, Chairman of the Midland Railway Company, who rented Pittodrie House and its shootings in Aberdeenshire for several seasons. Having observed the satisfactory working of this system in north east Scotland, he adopted this policy for the Midland Railway and soon all the other major companies followed suit. "*Second Class*" in the U.K. was consigned to history, at least for the time being.

On Thursday 8th January 1903 the Earl entertained the officials and working staff of the Joint Station, together with some staff of the Great North, to a dinner in the West End Café in Aberdeen. In an address to his guests the Earl recalled the railway arrangements in Aberdeen before the opening of the Joint Station in 1867. When returning to Haddo from school at Harrow near London, he experienced the "*annoyance*" of the transfer along the quay between Guild Street and Waterloo stations. He was jolted along in the omnibus worrying whether he would reach Waterloo in time for the north train connection – often the doors of the station were closed in the face of tardy transferring passengers! On one occasion the Earl set out to walk between the two stations as he returned home for the school holidays. When asked why he did not take the bus he always said that otherwise "*Bang goes saxpence*" which could remain in his pocket! He wore a large tall hat (as was the fashion then) which drew attention from a group of children who followed him along the quay, one wee girl pointing a scornful finger and shouting "*my grandpa, my grandpa*". He could only walk on, looking as dignified as possible.

Later, after the gathering had been joined by the Earl's second son The Hon. Dudley Gordon to loud cheering, in order to acknowledge "*the many acts of kindness on the part of his lordship*", the Earl and Countess were surprised to be presented with "*a handsome silver rose bowl to honour their silver wedding*". Mr R. A. Duguid, the Joint Station Superintendent, made the presentation and commented: "*We always claim your lordship as a neighbour; you are constantly amongst us; you live close to us, and many tokens of your kindness have been given to us, all of which have prompted the little gift which we offer to your lordship and Lady Aberdeen in name of the officers and staff of the Joint Station*". The rose bowl was inscribed: "*1903 Silver Wedding Gift to the Earl and Countess of Aberdeen from Officials and Staff at the Joint Station Aberdeen*".

The Earl paid tribute to the station management and staff and stated that he valued very highly the personal relationships he had forged at the station over the years. He also paid tribute to the guards and engine drivers of the Great North. The evening was concluded with musical entertainment, including by the world-famous fiddle player Scott Skinner. The Earl had taken care to be inclusive in his praise of all Great North employees and, therefore, it is of little surprise that on 19th January the following year (1904) Lord and Lady Aberdeen entertained the company's stationmasters to dinner at the same venue, the West End Cafe. However, on this occasion, it is believed to have been on the initiative of Lady Aberdeen (Lady Ishbel) who valued highly the service received from them. 130 guests attended.

THE PROJECT'S LEGACY

Interestingly, at this time the Great North broke new ground as one of the first railway companies to investing in road motor services (the Great North term for its buses, lorries, and char-a-bancs) with petrol-engine vehicles. A sub-committee was formed to take this initiative forward and a public meeting was held in Tarves in February 1904 which resulted in a petition to the Great North to start a bus service between Udny and Methlick – the same route for which Lord Aberdeen had proposed his railway back in 1879. The *Aberdeen Peoples Journal* of 25th June 1904 commented that the Udny to Methlick route was one of a number "*....through important agricultural localities left behind in the race of progress because of their distance from the existing railways. Light railways have long been talked of in the districts, but in their cases the motor car appears likely to beat the steel track, or at least (as local opinion will hope) to precede it.*" The same article reckoned that, with future development and improvement, in time "*....it may well be that in thinly populated districts the new vehicles will render the railway unnecessary and inaugurate a new era for rural life*". How prophetic this 1904 reporter was, although he could hardly have realised it at the time!

After a successful trial of 18hp Milnes-Daimler buses with a capacity of 18 passengers between Ballater Station and Braemar, two buses commenced the Udny Station – Methlick route on 15th November 1904. These were the start of quite a network of

GNSR motor bus SA73 outside Grant's paper shop in Methlick main street in the early years of the 20th century. Today the shop is a Costcutter store. The original mosaic flagstone incorporating the "Grant" name has been retained at the entrance.

(Aberdeen Transport Society)

Great North bus routes across the north east, with a central maintenance depot established at Kittybrewster. This was very likely a pre-emptive move to protect the railway company as times changed – perhaps the Great North now wished they had supported Lord Aberdeen's railway to Methlick all those years before! The Great North, in common with the Great Western Railway in England, pioneered hybrid vehicles in these early years which carried a bus or char-a-banc body in summer, whilst converting to a lorry in winter. The original fuel was benzol, a coal-tar by-product supplied by the Sandilands Chemical Works in Aberdeen, delivered in 40 gallon drums and decanted into two or four gallon cans before dispatch to Udny Station. Fuel consumption on the Udny – Methlick route was 8 miles per gallon. A local bus depot was established in Methlick in a timber-framed and roof-cladded shed which had been used by the previous horse-bus operator, Mr Davidson of Udny. It was rented for £12 per annum from a local

watchmaker, Mr Sinclair.

At first, the Methlick service managed to break even, but by July 1905 it was struggling and Mr William Deuchar, the Passenger Superintendent, reported: "*As the service is not paying by the present route it is recommended to run it by the public roads, Mr Deuchar to draw up a Timetable for approval shewing the First Car from Udny to run out of the 8.10am train from Aberdeen, running the morning and evening bus by the public road and a proposed Mid-day Service by Haddo House.*" A new service commenced on 1st August, combining mail carriage for the Post Office for £35 per annum and for Lord Aberdeen at £2 per annum. This additional revenue failed to improve matters; the mid-day service was withdrawn in October and the morning and evening buses were re-routed to run via Keithfield and Haddo House. However, by December the Great North's Traffic Committee was considering whether the Udny – Methlick service should be withdrawn. It resolved to

GNSR bus SA76 at Udny Station around 1905/6 with some of the station staff awaiting departure for Methlick. Note the large parcel on the platform and the single passenger. The bus was able to park next to the northbound platform, so that passengers arriving from Aberdeen could easily walk to it.   (GNSRA)

James Kerr of Methlick was one of the subsequent occupiers of the short-lived GNSR depot there. Here he is (on the right) standing in front of his already sizeable fleet at Methlick depot in 1922, with four of his drivers. James Chapman is the driver on the left, in front of 1922 Lancia bus SA5611. The other vehicles are (from left to right) SA4032, SA2643, SA4424, SA3003 and Kerr's first vehicle, SA2351, which was sold in March 1923. All were Ford T's except Fiat SA4424. Mr Kerr's House *Rockwood* is on the extreme left.   (Jean Sandison)

write to local landowners to inform them that, unless the decline in revenue was reversed, the service would be withdrawn. No improvement was reported in July 1906 and consideration was given as to a "*less expensive type*" of car. In October Lord Aberdeen's factor responded to a request for a revenue guarantee: "*It is hopeless to expect any of the residents to give a guarantee in connection with the running of the motor bus*". Perhaps this lack of enthusiasm reflected Lord Aberdeen's recent appointment as Lord Lieutenant of Ireland in December 1906 and his subsequent move to Dublin Castle. The result was the termination of the service at the end of December 1906 and the previous horse-drawn coach operator, Mr Davidson, agreed to resume (including the Methlick depot), but that service only lasted to 1908. It is unclear what happened after this, but the Great North was advertising a daily bus service between Methlick and Udny Station in its 1911 Working Timetable in a section entitled: "*Coaches not controlled by the Company, but announced by Owners to run in conjunction with Trains*". The morning service departed Methlick at 6.20am, called at Tarves

at 7.20am and arrived at Udny Station at 8.20am to connect with the 8.38am train to Aberdeen (7.05am ex Fraserburgh and 7.15am ex Peterhead, joining at Maud Junction and departing 7.58am). The return evening service departed Udny Station at 5pm after the arrival of the afternoon train from Aberdeen at 4.44pm. This train terminated at Ellon. The coach called at Tarves at 6pm and arrived in Methlick at 7pm, but it is not known if it called at Haddo. At an average speed of only 5¼ mph, it is likely that this service was still horse-drawn.

Later, in 1913, Lord Aberdeen chaired the Association for the Development of the Counties of Aberdeen, Kincardine and Banff, which was a pressure group pushing for light railway investment. However, Methlick did not regain its

It was very common for road carriers in the early 1920s to use vehicles as lorries on most days, but mount a bus body for passenger runs, echoing what the GNSR had done with several of its earliest vehicles, though possibly on a more frequent basis. James Kerr's RS3066 is carrying a full load to Methlick from Aberdeen while the driver, James Chapman, shows it off just north of the Bridge of Don. The lorry is carrying fish (in the basket on the cab roof), rolls of binder twine (for binding stooks of corn), a barrel of beer and a tea chest with loose tea.

(Jean Sandison)

motorised bus service until October 1915 when the Moffat Motor Company, based in the former Great North depot in Methlick and with offices in Gaelic Lane, Aberdeen, started operating a mail contract. On 1st March 1916 a full Aberdeen - Methlick bus service commenced via Mill of Fochel, Oldmeldrum and Newmacher.

After the First World War concluded, the Committee on Rural Transport (Scotland) convened in August 1918 to consider post-war policy and requirements. Five light railways were considered favourably and one of these was the Udny - Tarves - Methlick proposal. The Committee believed that light railways were a natural progression from successful road services. However, the Committee also clearly remembered the failure of the Great North's Methlick bus service in 1906 and commented: "*At present the district is served by a motor conveyance which is subsidised by the Post Office and makes two trips daily between Udny, Tarves and Methlick*". Nothing came of the light railway proposal, and events were by now moving towards the "Grouping" on 1st January 1923 and the demise of the Great North.

In 1918 the twice-daily mail and passenger bus service between Methlick and Udny was taken over by James Kerr, lessee of the Ythanview Hotel and sub-postmaster in Methlick. He extended the service on to Aberdeen via Tarves, Pitmedden and Whitecairns (initially on Mondays only) from

April 1921, continuing to operate out of the former Great North bus depot in the village. Originally from Maud, Kerr and his wife Elizabeth moved into an adjacent cottage called "Rockwood" which still exists today. It was a very informal service and one of his buses was involved in an amusing incident on 8th May 1926 when a car reversed out of a side road into its path. In the resulting court hearing the bus driver stated that "*a lady passenger seated on his right side....sounded the motor horn as they approached any side roads*". Asked why he allowed this, the driver continued: "*I was just letting her do it*", to which the sheriff responded: "*To give her something to do and keep her from talking, I suppose*". How delightfully politically incorrect!!

James Kerr claimed to be the first to drive a large bus into Aberdeen, and in the late 1920s his services expanded when his father transferred his bus business in Maud to him. In May 1928 Kerr was granted the licence to operate the main six-times daily Methlick – Aberdeen service. By 1931 he had added a service via Cairnorrie and one via Udny Green. Kerr established an Aberdeen base at 35 Dee Street where he had a waiting room and parcel office, with the Methlick service advertising "*passengers, luggage and small parcels*". A typical load from Aberdeen to Methlick in the 1920s comprised fresh fish, rolls of binder twine (for corn stooks), barrel of beer and a tea chest full of loose tea. Kerr continued the Great North practice of interchanging his vehicle bodies from bus to lorry. For example, on Fridays the lorry body was replaced with a bus body to allow local Methlick farmers to travel to the market in Aberdeen. On his death in 1936 Kerr's business passed initially to nominated trustees before being sold to James Sutherland (Peterhead) Limited in March 1943. This Company was in turn nationalised in 1950, coming under the control of Alexanders & Sons of Falkirk.

The Great North became part of the London & North Eastern Railway at the Grouping in 1923. The short line from Inverurie to Oldmeldrum had been the Great North's first branch and became the first to close to passengers, on 2nd November 1931, although freight was to continue to 1965. The branch which had served Haddo for 75 years was gone. It had the disadvantage of not providing a through service to Aberdeen, with passengers always having to change at Inverurie.

The Earl and the business of Haddo House and Estate continued to use Udny Station on the Buchan line. Although south of Ellon and despite a handful of other stations being closer to Haddo, Udny developed as the service centre for Udny Green, Pitmedden, Tarves and Methlick. Express trains took only 30 minutes to reach Aberdeen and even the slower trains arrived within 45 minutes. Udny's growing importance was reflected in the various proposed and actual transport links over the years. The village developed as a community around the railway station, which became its hub. That included the Station Hotel, originally owned by the Great North. It also served local sporting and agricultural estates. Passenger numbers were limited, but the station thrived on parcel and goods traffic, including seasonal game from Haddo Estate. Live incoming day-old chicks, racing pigeons, livestock, agricultural parts, seed potatoes (including from Pitmedden Estate), animal feed and so on made up the annual 12,000 tons of general goods traffic. The station also occasionally generated a degree of excitement when welcoming visiting celebrities and performers heading for concerts at Haddo House.

The 7th Earl had a distinguished public service career and his wife Lady Ishbel was greatly involved in charity work. In 1915 the Earl was created Marquess of Aberdeen and Temair (Temair being the ancient form of Tara, the old capital where the High Kings of Ireland held court before the 6th century). However, the Earl and Countess who dubbed themselves "*We Twa*", did not fare so well in some business ventures, especially in Canada, and it cost them dearly. Haddo Estate shrank from 75,000 acres in 1872 to 15,000 acres by the time of the 7th Earl's death in 1934. The sale of the entire Haddo Estate was considered in 1926. "*We Twa*" retired to Deeside and made Haddo over to their son George, 2nd Marquess (1879-1965). With no direct family, the estate passed on his death in 1965 into the hands of his younger brother Dudley, 3rd Marquess (1883-1972). This is Dudley Gordon who had joined his father at the Joint Station dinner which marked his parents' silver wedding all those years ago in 1903. He started his engineering career in Hall Russell's in Aberdeen and had a distinguished professional life. Apart from his appointments

as President of the Association of Refrigeration Engineers (1926-1929), President of the British Engineers Association (1936-1939) and President of the Federation of British Industries (1941-1943), the 3rd Marquess succeeded Oliver Bullied, Chief Mechanical Engineer of the Southern Railway, as President of the Institute of Mechanical Engineers in 1947 – another Haddo railway connection. He lived in Dartford in Kent and died in 1972.

As the years have rolled on there is one legacy which has survived to this day. The road from Aberdeen to Udny and on to Methlick via Udny Green, Pitmedden and Tarves is still a recognised bus route, and is operated by Stagecoach. Sadly, there is no stop for Haddo House.

Rockwood Cottage was the home of the early 20th century Methlick bus operator, James Kerr and his wife Elizabeth, and lies at the west end of the village beyond the cricket pitch. The bus depot was immediately adjacent (to the right) but has been demolished and replaced with this modern bungalow. After the Kerrs vacated Rockwood, the house became the office for the bus depot and the foreman lived there. Occasionally bus drivers slept in the house.

(Muick Gordon)

CONTINUING THE RAILWAY INTEREST

During the final year of the Second World War George, 2nd Marquess, made over Haddo Estate to his nephew, David Gordon with the full consent of his brother and heir Dudley. David, who was born in 1908, was Dudley's eldest son. He had lived at Haddo and had run the estate since 1946. On his father's death in 1972 he succeeded as 4th Marquess.

David continued the family interest in railways. He had, with the encouragement of his grandfather, started the family collection of model trains in his youth in the 1920s. He remembered his grandfather telling him about his Udny – Methlick railway proposal and mused that, had it been built, it would have been a wonderful line for steam. However, he realised that his musings were "*castles in the air*", but that one consolation was that the Haddo Estate still had "*a very contented tenantry*".

The 4th Marquess was able to indulge his interest in railways during the Second World War when he commanded the 2nd Company of the Gordon Highlanders. He and his 400 troops were stationed for field training at

Several railway models are included in the collection at Haddo House, mostly dating from the early years of the twentieth century. This one is of a much earlier locomotive dating from the 1850s or 1860s although it is not known when the model was built. The motor bus in the background is modelled on a pre-First World War London bus, close to the era of Kerr's buses.   (Muick Gordon, courtesy National Trust for Scotland)

Cruden Bay Hotel, which was requisitioned in August 1940. Over the following winter he commuted to the hotel daily from Bucksburn, changing at Ellon to catch the 6.50am goods train to Boddam and riding in the brake van. One of his Company's jobs was to keep the railway line at Cruden Bay clear of the heavy snow which fell that winter.

David Gordon's love of railways, and of the Great North in particular, led him into membership of the Great North of Scotland Railway Association until his death in 1974. He loved railways and he loved talking about railways. He practiced what he preached and travelled widely by train. His enthusiasm

rubbed off on his wife June, Lady Aberdeen, and his son Andrew. The family's favourite locomotive class was Sir Nigel Gresley's streamlined A4, especially *Mallard*, holder of the world steam speed record, and today in preservation in the National Railway Museum in York. The 4th Marquess left one final comment about his grandfather's proposed railway. He thought that even the final estimated cost of £80,000 would have been too low. He was probably right!

The family collection of vintage model trains is stored within Haddo House which is run by the National Trust for Scotland. Some of the models are on display.

These are among the interesting models on display at Haddo House. The early steam locomotive illustrated on the previous page is at the back. In front of it on the upper level are the London General omnibus, a rudimentary timber wagon and a London & South Western full brake coach. At the front is a K3 class locomotive. Originally designed by Sir Nigel Gresley for the Great Northern Railway, he developed the class for the LNER. This is a faithful representation of the LNER design, except for the tender. The discoloration under the boiler shows that it is a live steam model.   (Muick Gordon, courtesy National Trust for Scotland)

Sources and Bibliography

Aberdeen Evening Express

Aberdeen Free Press

Aberdeen Journal

Edinburgh Gazette

David Fasken and David Spaven, *Aberdeen to Elgin and Inverness, The Insider Rail Guide,* (Kessock Books 2017)

Peter Fletcher, *Directors, Dilemmas And Debt* (GNSRA and HRS 2010)

Great North of Scotland Railway Association, *Great North Memories* (Vol 2)

Great North *Reviews* Nos 46 & 81

Haddo Estate Archive (courtesy Lord Aberdeen)

Keith Jones, *The Earl of Aberdeen and the Joint Station – a 1903 Celebration* (GNSRA, *Great North Review*, Vol 54, No 215, 2017)

Duncan McLeish, *Rails to Banff, Macduff and Oldmeldrum* (GNSRA 2014)

Janet M. McLeman, *Walking The Line* (GNSRA 2015)

Mike Mitchell, *Great North of Scotland Railway Road Services 1854 – 1930* (GNSRA 2016)

National Trust for Scotland, *Haddo House* (NTS Guide, revised 2013)

Anne-Mary Paterson, *Pioneers of the Highland Tracks* (Highland Railway Society 2010)

David Ross, *The Great North of Scotland Railway (*Stenlake Publishing 2015)

Alan H. Sangster, *The Story and Tales of the Buchan Line* (Oxford Publishing Co., 1983)

John Thomas and David Turnock, *A Regional History of the Railways of Great Britain*, Volume 15, North of Scotland (House of Lochar, 1989)

Lord and Lady Aberdeen and Temair, *We Twa* : reminiscences, published W. Collins Sons & Co Ltd, 1925. An online version is available from the Hathi Trust.

H. A. Vallance, *The Great North of Scotland Railway* (House of Lochar, 1988)

Great North of Scotland Railway Association

Founded 1964

The Association caters for all those interested in the history of the Great North of Scotland Railway and its constituent companies, as well as the lines during the LNER, British Railways and post-privatisation periods. The Association promotes the study and collection of information, documents and illustrations relating to all aspects of the North East's railways. It also facilitates and co-ordinates members' research and provides information for modellers.

Members receive a quarterly *Review* containing articles, photographs, drawings and news of the railway, both historical and current. The Association has produced a comprehensive range of books and technical papers covering aspects of the railway in great detail. Members have access to an extensive photographic and drawing archive. Members receive a discount on Association publications. Meetings and excursions are regularly organised.

For further information, please look at the Association's website

www.gnsra.org.uk